The Bloodred Tree

The Bloodred Tree

Before the Flood

JOHN C. STRINGER

RESOURCE *Publications* • Eugene, Oregon

THE BLOODRED TREE
Before the Flood

Copyright © 2011 John C. Stringer. All rights reserved. Except for brief quotations in critical publications or reviews, no part of this book may be reproduced in any manner without prior written permission from the publisher. Write: Permissions, Wipf and Stock Publishers, 199 W. 8th Ave., Suite 3, Eugene, OR 97401.

Resource Publications
An Imprint of Wipf and Stock Publishers
199 W. 8th Ave., Suite 3
Eugene, OR 97401
www.wipfandstock.com

ISBN 13: 978-1-60899-874-6

Manufactured in the U.S.A.

All scripture quotations, unless otherwise indicated, are taken from the Holy Bible, New International Version®, NIV®. Copyright ©1973, 1978, 1984 by Biblica, Inc.™ Used by permission of Zondervan. All rights reserved worldwide.

Epigraph, with acknowledgement to my friend Kay Rothman, Manhatten, N.Y.

Map of the Great Plain © John C. Stringer

The Orders of the Cherubim © John C. Stringer

West Light and East Light © John C. Stringer

Nemrut Dag excavation site map © John C. Stringer

Archaeological cross section map © John C. Stringer

All other illustrations of creatures and people © Kees Bruin, Sumner, New Zealand.

*To Asher, James and Alex,
my own Jahf, Hamaa and Sem;
still building our ship together . . .*

What I am about to tell you is a lie,
But everything in it is absolutely true.

Contents

Acknowledgments ix
Maps, Guides, and Illustrations xi
Preface xxi

1. Discord 1
2. Tracks 3
3. Michael's Wrath 8
4. Moses' Coffee Pots 19
5. Shemgazi and the Bloodred Tree 26
6. The Cube 43
7. Kainos and the Red Death 50
8. The Affluveum Codex 58
9. The Nephaliim come forth 63
10. Evil Men and the Breaking of the Earth 76
11. Andraemon and Fafnir-Amon 87
12. Nu of Van 98
13. The Nephaliim of Nu 108
14. Men come against the Great Ship 122
15. Tears from Heaven 131
16. The Simulcast 137
17. The Nephaliim Undone 139
18. Epilogue 148

Glossary 149

Acknowledgments

Special thanks to my conceptual readers: my wife Laurie, in New Zealand; Rachel Hills in Perth, Australia; my copy editor Gerri Maynard (Maple) in Toronto, Canada (http://gerrimaynard.word press.com) and the editorial and marketing teams at Wipf & Stock in Eugene, Oregon, who backed my proposal from the beginning without question.

Maps, Guides, and Illustrations

The Great Plain, first–tenth generations	xii, 66–67
The Orders of the Cherubim	xiii
War in the Gates of Heaven	xiv
The Generations of Men	xv
Some of the Hu-Man Tribes of the Earth	xvi
The Nemrut Dag excavation site 1961–1988	xvii
Archaeological cross section, 'Track Alley' tunnel complex	xviii
The Life of Vitruvius Affluveum	xix
The Wall Glyph	24
'The Hilltop Strangler' Glyph	44
The Algaroi or Ceratopsia	70
A spiked Styracs	71
Raptormen	72
Alsoi and Ankylosoi	73
Fafnir-Amon	84
A marine crypto-clidfoi grabbing a flying pteradon	119

xii *Maps, Guides, and Illustrations*

i. The Great Plain, first–tenth generations

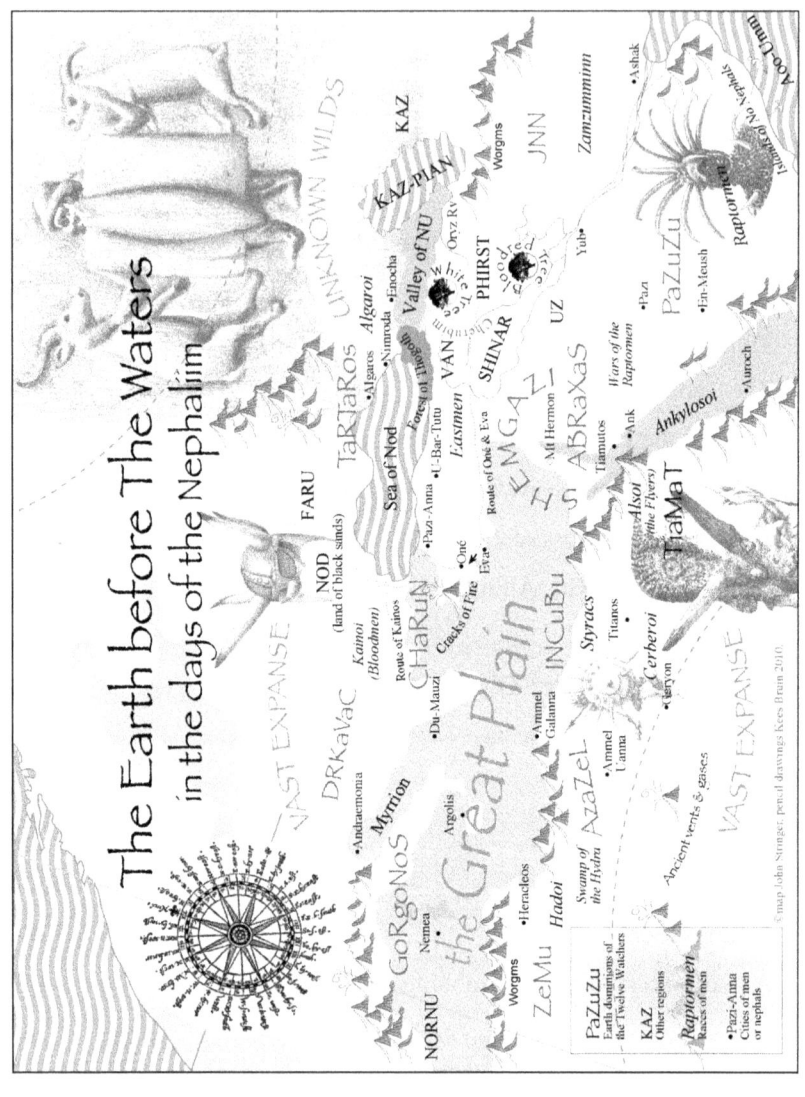

Maps, Guides, and Illustrations xiii

ii. The Orders of the Cherubim

The Orders of the Cherubim

Under each Prince within each gate are arrayed four Orders each of seraphim and teraphim: Song, Warriors, Words and Watching. 32 Orders around the Throne.

xiv *Maps, Guides, and Illustrations*

iii. War in the Gates of Heaven

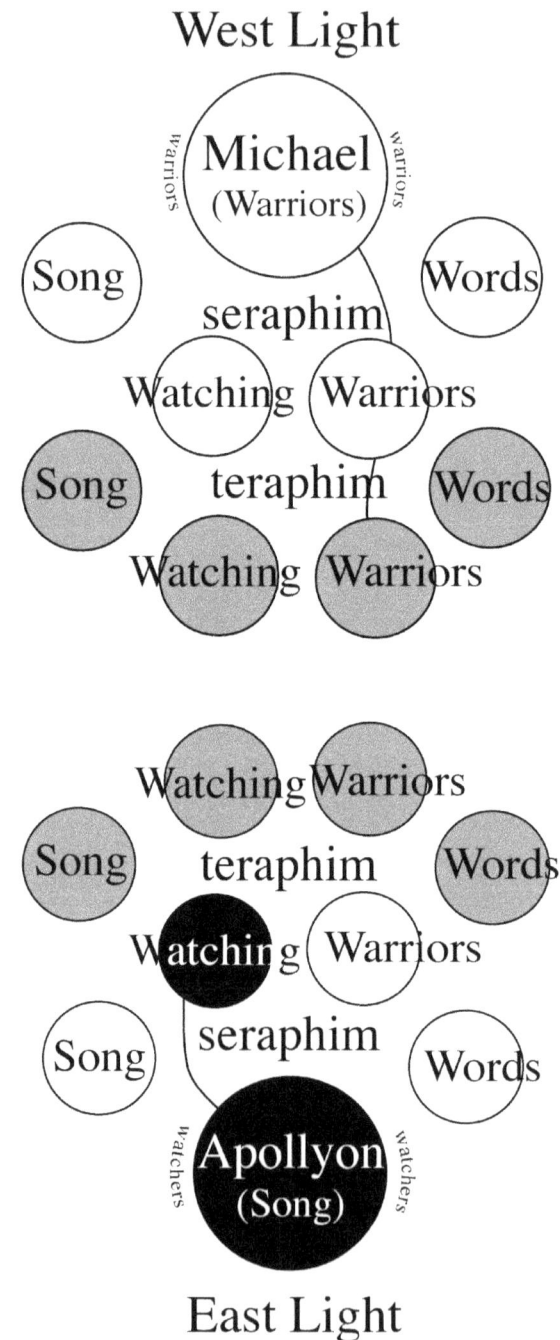

iv. The Generations of Men

Phirst and Onés	Chief Hu-Man of the Great Plains
1. Oné [Onay]	
2. Kainos, A-Bel	
3. En-Ocha *	3. Al-Algar/Nim-Roda (of the North)
4. Methu-Saleh	4. Ammel-Uanna (in the South)
5. Lam-Ech	5. Ammel-Galanna (from the West)
6. Nu	6. Du-Mauzi
7. Jahf, Hamaa and Sem	7. En-Meush-Um-Galanna
8. ... and their sons	8. Ensi-Pazi-Anna
9 .... for	9. Enme-Du-Ranki
10 ... three generations	10. U-Bar-Tutu/Zi-U-Sudra (the last)
* the generation of Andraemon of the Myrrion	(Eastern and Western peoples)

v. Some of the Hu-Man Tribes of the Earth
    Algaroi/Ceratopsia
    Alsoi
    Ankylosoi
    Andraemonoi
    Cerboroi
    Eastmen
    Hemenoi
    Hadoi
    Kainoi
    Men of Oné
    Men of Phirst
    Nu-oi
    Raptormen
    Styracs
    Zamzummin

Maps, Guides, and Illustrations xvii

vi. The Nemrut Dag excavation site 1961–1988

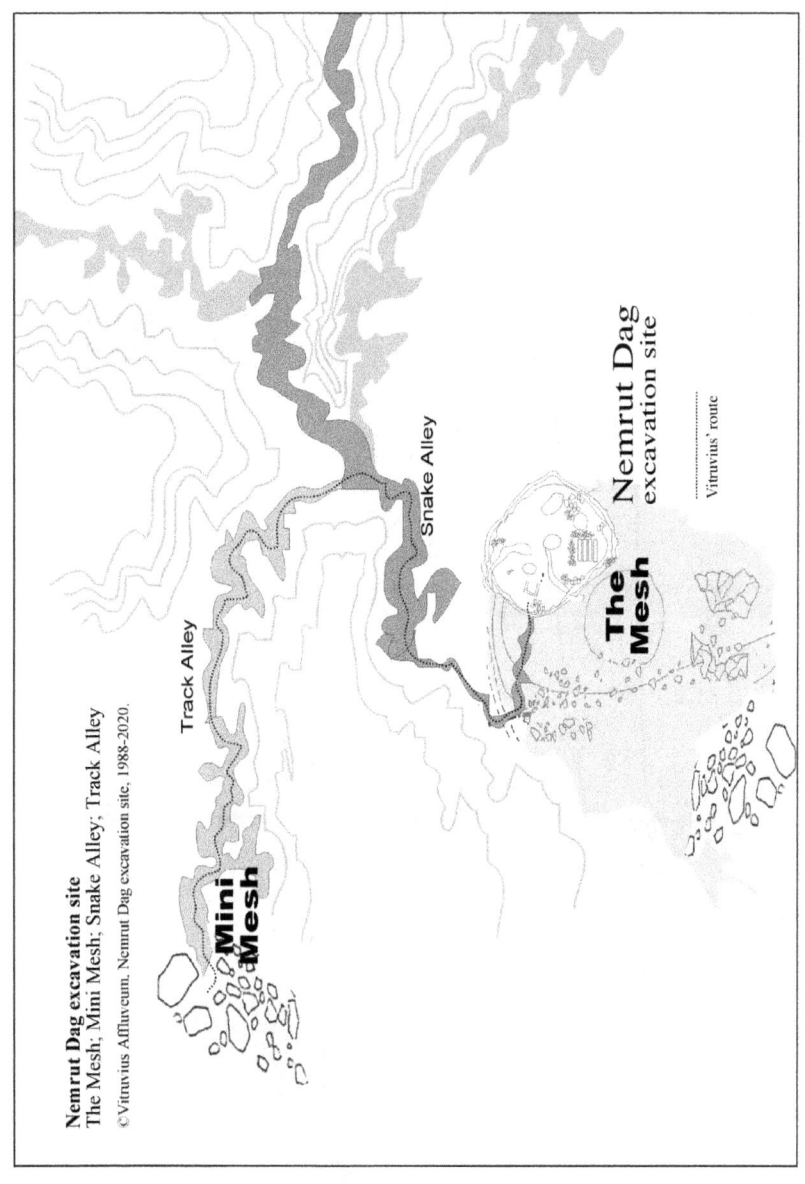

xviii *Maps, Guides, and Illustrations*

vii. Archaeological cross section, 'Track Alley' tunnel complex

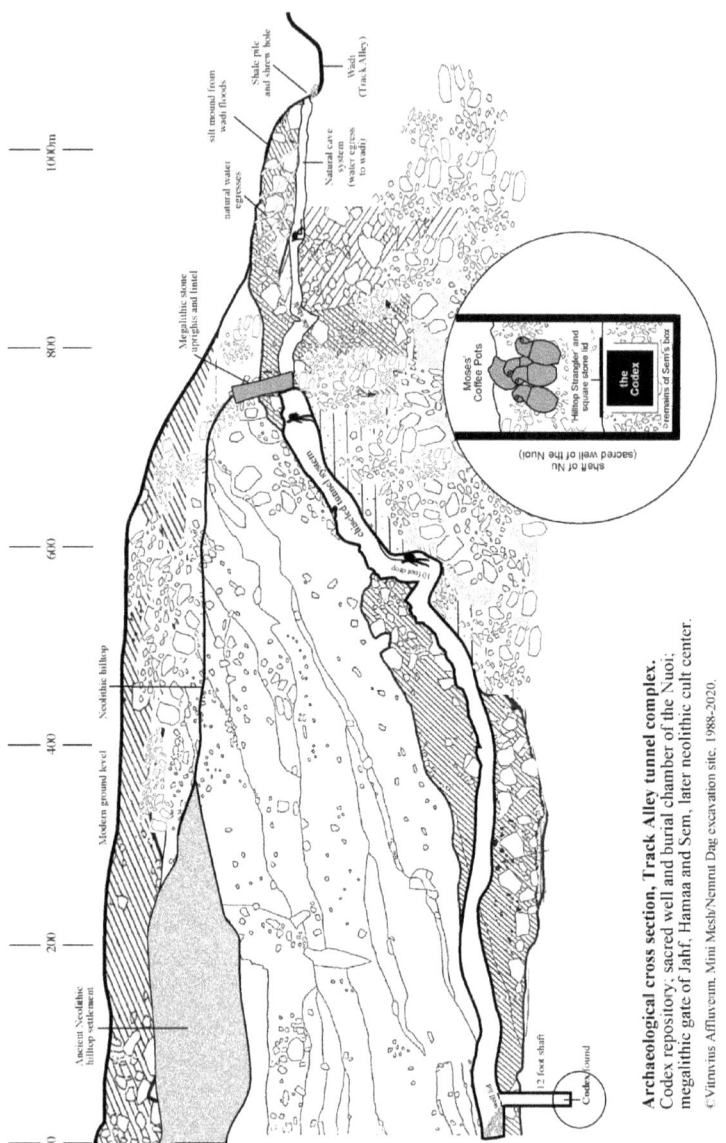

Archaeological cross section, Track Alley tunnel complex. Codex repository; sacred well and burial chamber of the Nuoi; megalithic gate of Jahf; Hamaa and Sem, later neolithic cult center.

©Vitruvius Affluveum, Mini Mesh/Nemrut Dag excavation site. 1988-2020.

viii. The Life of Vitruvius Affluveum

0	Born	1938
17–20	(4 years) undergrad/masters	1955–58
20–22	Doctoral thesis	1958–60
22,23	Dig site research and post grad study	1960,61
23–50	(27 years) major dig, Nemrut Dag	1961–1988
50	Finds tracks/urns and Codex	1988
50–82	(32 years) team decoding Codex	1988–2020
82	All-Nations Vatican simulcast	2020
84	Dies in Adelaide, Australia	2022

Preface

We begin by telling children stories,
Which, taken as a whole are fiction,
Though they contain some truth.

—Socrates to Plato, *The Republic*

Art is a lie
That helps us understand
The truth

—Picasso

A WORD ABOUT POETRY, IMAGINATION AND 'THE DARK SIDE.'

This story is a fiction, but the Bible is my source, which I believe is true. By "true" I mean that the Bible is divinely inspired and reliable, contains poetry, prose, metaphor, simile, hyperbole and stories. Jesus was great at stories. Maybe that is why the Bible is the best selling book of all time, way ahead of the Babylonian *Epic of Gilgamesh* or *The Republic* of Plato.

J. R. R. Tolkien, another person who was good at stories, once said about imaginative story telling (what he called "fairytales"),

> "We have come from God, and inevitably the myths woven by us, though they contain error, will also reflect a splintered fragment of the true light, the eternal truth that is with God. Indeed, only by myth-making, only by becoming a 'sub-creator' and inventing stories, can Man [sic] aspire to the state of perfection that he knew before the Fall. Our myths may be misguided, but they steer however shakily towards the true Harbour."[1]

1. Tolkien cited in Smith, *A Closer Look at the Lord of the Rings,* Kingsway, 2002, p. 13.

In his book *Epic*, John Eldredge wrote,

> "When we were born, we were born into the midst of a great story begun before the dawn of time. A story of adventure, of risk and loss, heroism . . . and betrayal. A story where good is warring against evil, danger lurks around every corner, and glorious deeds wait to be done. Think of all those stories you've ever loved —there's a reason they stirred your heart. They've been trying to tell you about the true Epic ever since you were young."

As a pastor I have little time for religious Christians who struggle with *Harry Potter* simply because it has wizards in it. All I can say is, what then to do with: C.S. Lewis' White Witch, his talking lion, and the satyrs of Narnia? Professor Tolkien's resurrected wizard Gandalf the white? Or the demons, dragons, fire balls, lions, giants, and howling Doleful Creatures of John Bunyan's *Pilgrim's Progress*? Lewis, Tolkien and Bunyan were all devoted Christians *and* great storytellers.[2] Then of course there's the matter of the Witch of Endor (not the *Star Wars* Endor) in 1 Samuel 28 conjuring one of the Bible's greatest prophets from the dead. Perplexing! (But only for those living in small worlds of their own constriction).

Put simply, the God I serve is imaginative beyond description and his creativity knows no bounds. His truth is expressed in the diversity of color, shape and form that make up the universe surrounding us, including things we cannot even imagine. My God made foxes that fly, spiders that fish, birds that swim under water, fish that live on land, bats that echo-locate, and beetles that shoot fire. "The heavens declare the glory of God; the skies proclaim the work of his hands," Psalm 19:1 exuberantly declares. Who could not enjoy a God, "the Maker of the Bear and Orion, the Pleiades and the constellations of the south?" (Job 9:9). The Holy Bible and Shrek have one thing in common—a donkey that speaks (Numbers 22).

The point is, that art, creativity, and imagination are just as important as "facts." How is love truly conveyed without poetry, or the wind or the desert without song? There are facets of our universe that can only be approached obliquely, with nuance 'through a looking glass

---

2. Professor Tolkien was, of course, largely responsible for Lewis' conversion from ambivalent agnosticism to practical Christianity (one of the greatest writers of the twentieth-century responsible for one of the greatest theological apologists of the twentieth-century), converting Lewis to, not Tolkien's beloved Catholicism, but Lewis' adopted Protestantism. Creativity and colour at work again!

darkly," to quote Lewis Carroll (*Alice in Wonderland*) paraphrasing Paul (1 Corinthians 13:12). Perhaps Picasso put it best, "Art is a lie that helps us understand the truth."

Oscar Wilde said that Art, like Nature, has its monsters, indicating the need humanity has to create monsters (vampires, dragons, bogy men) parallel to nature's creative reality (vampire bats, komodo dragons, silver back gorillas). The Bible speaks of monsters figuratively (Revelation) as well as literally (Job 40). Monsters clearly serve a mythological purpose, but actually also exist.[3]

As I wrote this story, I wrestled with "the dark side." Much of its darkness, however, pales into insignificance compared to the psychopathic depravity of real history: the Spanish Inquisition; the Brazen Bull; the Iron Maiden; the sadism of Phalaris, Tyrant of Agrigentum; or Vlad Dracul Tepes III of Wallencia following in the spirit of Assyrian cruelty. I drew many of the details of this fiction from the pages of ancient history. If you find this tale dark, read about the real world in which some people have lived. Into that wretched darkness comes a gracious and loving God with a lighted torch. And that is a central premise for this work. If you believe there was a real flood, as I do, we have to understand why God destroyed everything he had made. It must have been terrible. No one really talks about that, so I do. I believe a malevolent spiritual force entered creation and sought to steal or ruin man's created destiny. The "violence" spoken of in Genesis six was seen and unseen, as concerned with microscopic truths as much as whole populations. Without intervention, the earth and everything in it was doomed to a slow and destructive hell-on-earth; and so God acted, to redeem and ultimately glorify. I seek not only to portray how things might have been, but to discuss how God could have been working a perfect redemptive purpose through human and angelic freewill, without violating either, before both of us ruinously polluted everything 'that was good.'

The idea of the nephaliim ("nephilim") is not mine; it actually comes from the Bible. Three theories exist among scholars about the nature of the beings described in the sixth chapter of Genesis: royalty or aristocrats distinguished from mere peasants; the descendants of Seth in contrast to the descendants of Cain; or thirdly, actual fallen angels 'marrying' human women to generate a hybrid race. As bizarre and

---

3. Of note in this respect is the publication *Dragons, A Natural History* (1995) by two serious zoological scholars, Dr Karl Shujer and Dr Desmond Morris (*The Naked Ape*).

'sci-fi fantastic' as the latter seems–easily the most peculiar of the three explanations–among the serious theologians I have read, it is the third explanation (fallen angel) that attracts the most solid position.[4] The Hebrew etymology of "nephilim" alone is revealing and the start point. Fallen angels and women were the view of the early church fathers as well as the translators of the Septuagint (the Greek Old Testament from ancient Hebrew) as well as the ancient rabbis. So, the actual existence of Nephilim has theological pedigree. Marry that to parallel themes (demi-gods, god-men, gods coming down) in the religious mythology of other cultures from the earliest of times, and an interesting hypothesis emerges underpinning the 'fiction' you hold in your hand.

We can only begin to imagine what the world of angels is like. There are hints in the Bible. Like us, angels are created beings, but they exist in a different dimension. We're not sure when they were made. They have the ability to cross between their world and ours, can eat food, fight, talk, and fly.[5] They belong to the created order as we do, but are quite different, and can see into our created dimension. They don't understand some things, such as God's intentions and interactions with mankind. In time, humans too, will be like angels physically (if that is the right word). Our promised transformation (something denied angels) coalesces both the physical and spiritual dimensions without diminishing either. In this sense we are blessed, as humans will experience both worlds. This has interesting implications for God's statement that he will create both a new earth as well as a new heaven. "Heaven" is never a diminishment of physicality or the earth. I understand it this way, "God loves trees" and they will always be (just read Ezekiel 47 and Revelation 22 side-by-side, separated by over 600 years).

Jesus is uniquely the ultimate man, the "first born from the dead" (the "One" the nephaliim fear so much in this story). He was the first human to have been birthed, to have died, and then come alive again using the same body to walk through walls, yet eat, be invisible, and yet retain the scars inflicted on his physical flesh. He is both man and God and promises that we too will one day be 'gods,' that is, humans who have angelic reality in the footsteps and likeness of Jesus himself (Psalm 82:6 as well as John 10 and Luke 20).

4. For a quality summarising discussion, see Dr. Chuck Missler's *Textual Controversy: Mischievous Angels or Sethites?* http://www.khouse.org/articles/1997/110.

5. Job 1:7; Genesis 18:8; Joshua 5:13; Luke 1:19; Judges 13:20 respectively.

"I said, 'You are "gods;" you are all sons of the Most High,'" Psalm 82:6.

"Jesus answered them, 'Is it not written in your Law, "I have said you are gods"'? If he called them 'gods,' to whom the word of God came—and the Scripture cannot be broken—what about the one whom the Father set apart as his very own and sent into the world? Why then do you accuse me of blasphemy because I said, 'I am God's Son'?" John 10.

> "... and they can no longer die; for they are like the angels. They are God's children, since they are children of the resurrection."
> Luke 20.

In this novel, I have arranged heavenly angels into hierarchical orders.

Around the throne of God are Four Great Creatures, Four Great Princes (archangels who are also "cherubim") and twenty-four Elders.

The Four Great Princes preside over four "Lights:" The North, South, West and East Lights that are also the great Gates of heaven. They are Michael, Gabriel, Raphael and Apollyon, in-keeping (in part) with hints from Christian tradition.

Michael certainly is an archangel (Jude 9) and "a great prince" (Daniel 12:1). Gabriel, as God's principal mouthpiece, 'stands in the presence of God' (Luke 1:19). Satan was a "guardian cherub" (Ezekiel 28:14), but I have demoted him here to seraphim status, and raise up another who is mentioned in Revelation 9:11 as the angel of destruction. The differing nature, or function, of angels is probably no more than the differing nature of people, with varying gifts, weaknesses and strengths. At best it is complex and an expression of God's infinite creativity.

Around the four cherubim—the four archangels in their respective gates—are a host of lessor angels: seraphim followed by teraphim.

Each of the great Gates, or "Lights," governed by an archangel, has a distinctive ethos. Michael is of "Warriors." Gabriel is of "Words," Raphael "Watching," and Apollyon "Song." It is the Light of Song that comes unstuck in our story, that is, the music of heaven.

Around each separate archangel within each Gate is a second order of angels, great seraphim. They are also grouped in the four ethoi. Around Raphael for example, in the North Light of Watching, are also seraphim of Warriors, Song, Words and Watching. This means that each of the archangels is supported within their Gate by aspects of each of the other Gates. Each distinctive ethos (Song, Words) is made up of complementary aspects of heaven in perfect unity and enhancement. Each Light is made up of smaller additional portions of all the others. Michael for example, when he comes against Song, gathers not only all the Warrior orders from his West Gate (of Warriors) but also calls on all the Warrior seraphim and teraphim from the other Gates, the Warriors of Watching, and the Warriors of Words, and so on. Similarly, Raphael (Watching) might be able to call on the Watching seraphim or teraphim from Gabriel's Gate (Words) or Michael's Gate (Warriors). It is essentially Apollyon's disorder in usurping Raphael's function, seeking to Watch Unos and interact with creation, when he is the archangel of Song given a heavenly function around the Throne that begins the unravelling of his Gate.

Around the seraphim of each Gate is a third order of angels, attending teraphim. They too are arranged in the four ethoi: as Warriors, Song, Watching and Words, a quarter of each around each gate.

Four archangels at the gates of heaven;

Four Great Creatures around the Throne;

Twenty-four Elders (six amounts of four) also around the Throne, representing the three orders of creation: angel, humankind, and animals.

Seraphim around them in four orders made up of four parts each.

Teraphim around them in four orders made up of four parts each.

Three orders of angels, in descending divisions, billions of beings.

When Apollyon falls, he deceives the Watching seraphim of his Gate who have shared the knowledge of man and Unos' ministry on the earth. Their special duty was Watching. The other East Gate seraphim of Song, Warriors and Words fight against Michael too, subservient to their Lord Apollyon, but are subdued. The four orders of teraphim of the East Gate all submit, but are murdered by Apollyon and the East Gate seraphim, particularly the Watcher seraphim of Song.

Shemgazi (an ancient name of Lucifer) is one of these murdering seraphim of Watching of the East Gate (a "murderer from the beginning" as Jesus said) under his overlord Apollyon, the archangel of Song.

After the East Gate archangel Apollyon and the rebellious seraphim are bound in the Yawning Abyss, Shemgazi, by direct appeal to the Throne, is freed with a small remnant (just twelve seraphim, representing the months of the year and the later tribes of Israel).

Michael hurls the twelve seraphim, direct participants in the mass murder, to the earth in great carnage. There is a common tradition of this among the ancient peoples of the world and I find it fascinating that Genesis represents this as well. Always "the gods" came down, usually after war in the heavens; and things got bad on earth. They went by various names: Igigi, Anunnaki, Watchers, Titans, gods of Olympus, Quatzequatl, Ea, Enki.

In this story, six of the seraphim Watchers gain an ability to interact with the physical world (six is the number of man). They are the "Watchers of Flesh." Without authority, they father the nephaliim with female humanity (Genesis six). The other six seraphim Watchers are spiritual entities only. All twelve, under Shemgazi's governance, spread out across the globe (at this time one massive landmass surrounded by water, see map) and govern territorial areas with authority over humanity beneath them. (This territorial hierarchy is completely disrupted by the Flood). The Sa-Tan establishes his throne at the very center, where men have begun. The Watchers also preside over animals, which have spread more quickly than man, and have to wait until men spread across the earth and come under their territorial influence. The Flesh Watchers interact with women in their dominions, and so into these geographical places are born small numbers of regional nephaliim.

Andraemon's home, for example, falls within the dominion of GoRgoNos who is not a Flesh Watcher. It is therefore a long time before a nephaliim spawned by a neighbouring Flesh Watcher wanders into the Myrrion, secluded for some time from the influence of these terrible creatures birthed by Flesh Watchers elsewhere on the earth in their dominions.

By their nature, the nephaliim are physical creatures, bound by physicality and geography unlike their fathers the Watchers, who are restricted only by their relationships with each other territorially, and the governance of their master, who has become their de facto 'archangel' of a dark earth Gate to whom they have surrendered their power.

The Flesh Watchers and their six seraphim kin can only interact with the earth by influencing men and by birthing nephaliim–a direct vehicle of influence. That is why the corruption of the kings of men is so vital. This corruption is the cause of the many wars, as Watchers complete with each other through the chief Hu-Mans (the kings of men) to control each other's tracts of soil, like hyenas at a waterhole. Sa-Tan is bent on controlling the whole earth. The nephaliim are an attempt to counterfeit men (seen in so many instinctive fantasy epics from the Matrix *agents*, to Star Trek's *borg*, Tolkien's *uruks* and *uruk-hai*, to the 'rage zombies' of *Legend*, *28 Days Later* and *28 Weeks Later*, etc). The purpose is to subdue the earth with a counter race of physical beings, godless spawn outside the created order, but using the spirit within man to create life.

It is this mental and moral corruption of men—and the widespread destructive war violence that results over ten generations—as well as the more sinister genetic corruption of men, land animals and birds (as nephaliim and mutated beasts) that causes God to destroy the dry earth with water as an act of mercy towards creation. God's purpose is to redeem creation and to raise-up his own ultimate kingdom of incorruptible flesh-spirit (human) sons, for whom the whole of creation was intended.

> "The creation waits in eager expectation for the sons of God to be revealed. For the creation was subjected to frustration, not by its own choice, but by the will of the one who subjected it, in hope that the creation itself will be liberated from its bondage to decay and brought into the glorious freedom of the children of God. We know that the whole creation has been groaning as in the pains of childbirth right up to the present time. Not only so, but we ourselves, who have the first fruits of the Spirit, groan inwardly as we wait eagerly for our adoption as sons, the redemption of our bodies." Romans 8:19–22.

> "Since the children have flesh and blood, he too shared in their humanity so that by his death he might destroy him who holds the power of death—that is, the devil—Hebrews 2:14.

These are things that angels have longed to look into and understand. I hope this drop of ink, to paraphrase Byron, encourages you to think.

Research is a good thing, so before you start, there are some *Maps, Guides and Illustrations* immediately ahead of this *Preface*—a helpful reference index while reading. The *Glossary* at the end may also help un-package some of the difficult names, places and creatures you come across as you read.

John C. Stringer
Christchurch, New Zealand.

1

Discord

In whose heart is perverseness,
Who deviseth evil continually,
Who soweth discord.

—Proverbs 6:14

Darkness took me . . . In those black depths . . .
I felt the call of ancient anger and the claws
Of undying sorrow. . . . There lingers the
Taint of his touch and the shadows of the
First hosts to ever chant his Evil Songs.

—J. R. R. Tolkien, Lord of the Rings

A translation of the Affluveum Codex, by the international scholars of Bletchley Park II, Istanbul Conservatory, Affluveum Institute. English version, The Vatican simulcast, 2020.

THERE WAS SILENCE IN heaven for God had ceased from all his work. The sons of God, all the heavenly creatures, and the Twenty-Four Elders that were to be, were in awe at everything God had made.

On the eighth day the symphony of his presence refreshed and went out into the heavens. The music rose and plunged like heaving currents in the deepest ocean and began to peak towards a crescendo. It swelled through the deepness of space and filled the entire earth. The melody echoed beneath the canopy of the trees, amongst countless myriads of colored leaves and across vast swathes of breathing green. It gloried in the commuting of foaming gushing waters that fed the lakes and watercourses where giant behemoths and brontosauroi lazed and fed. In the skies above it sang beneath the wings of giant pterosaurs; it was heard deep in the veins of the earth where rock flowed like liquid gold nursing the earth and warming her skin.

The Cherubim and the Four Creatures worshipped God and led the hosts of seraphim and teraphim in song. The praise was continuous, swelling and beautiful beyond the imagination of man, who worked quietly and peacefully in the fruit garden God had planted in the land of Phirst west of Kaz-Pian.

The man Oné [Onay] and the beasts of the earth were at peace. Eva lived in unity with Oné and they loved and worked together, naked, and transparent before Unos, the LoGoi ,when he came calling among the trees. Unos called often into the earth, each seventh day, to talk with, laugh with, and teach the man and the woman. This went on for a long season; fellowship on the earth between God and man, music in heaven, worship and peace, until . . .

. . . a discordant note was heard in the seventh heaven.

2

Tracks

When you set out on your journey to Ithaca,
Pray that the road is long,
Full of adventure, full of knowledge.

—Constantine Peter Cavafy.

A bend in the road is only the end
If you choose not to turn the corner.

It took him twenty-seven years.

The early years of Dr. Vitruvius Affluveum's archaeological dig at Nemrut Dag on the western edge of Lake Van (1961–1988), Turkey, had consumed every waking moment. From the initial research following his doctoral thesis in 1960; to the discovery of the documents about the Hierothesion of Antiochus I Epiphanes in the Vatican in 1961; the topographical survey of the tumulus and surrounding district in 1962; to the directing of the layout and early discoveries of artifacts through 1965, had fed his passion. The collation and illustration of the artifacts, the writing up of the findings, and the endless discussions with colleagues wrestling with conclusions, had been the grist to a vibrant archaeological career.

In the first decade of excavation at Nemrut Dag, Vitruvius had unearthed an agricultural settlement. He deduced it had become established as part of the trade in obsidian from north Armenia. A wealth of striking first-century BC broken artifacts jumbled within the compacted colluveum had steadily emerged from the pain-staking dig.

Twenty seven years on, 1988, and aged 50, with no significant new discoveries, and finances rapidly coming to an end, Vitruvius was depressed. He had withdrawn into the minutiae of his field notebooks and academic papers. The occasional guest lectureship abroad brought a welcome change of scene but inside he was spent. The dried pottery shards uncovered in the first seasons of excavation littered his shelves like mocking ghouls. Increasingly, he had buried himself in books about his childhood heroes: Champollion, Layard, Schliemann, Evans, and Carter.[1]

An ever-present malaise, tinged with a gnawing restlessness, chewed at his soul on this torpid evening. He snapped shut the little hardback on the life of Flavio Biondo, fine dust ballooning up into the air, and tossed the book carelessly onto the tumbling pile beside his couch. Melancholy drew him outside to the cool night air beneath the glorious sweep of the the Milky Way.

For a half hour or so he walked aimlessly around the dig–known affectionately as 'the Mesh' (after Gilgamesh). Vitruvius occasionally stooped to inspect a pebble, a bone or any other item that caught his interest; the skills of his chosen vocation were not completely dormant. But the motivation had long departed. He just no longer cared, instead the man felt like a fossil fused in a petrified forest.

Coming to the northern edge of the Mesh, he dropped down into the dry wadi. It wound like a contorting snake around the rock outcrops pockmarking the ancient seabed scarp he had first identified as interesting all those years ago. A brace of small quail scuttled down the sandy trail of 'Snake Alley' as the seasonal volunteers had labelled it. He followed, distractedly gazing up at the night sky. It was dark, and fireflies traced dances through the cooling night air.

Vitruvius had been walking awhile in the moonlight when he noticed unusual animal tracks crossing his path in the sand laid down after the most recent sand storm. He checked himself his interest aroused, turned, and followed them.

They belonged to some breed of small quadruped but he didn't recognise the paw prints. The tracks proceeded down the sandy tributary off to his left for a few hundred yards or more, before disappearing up onto a pile of collapsed shale beneath the overhang of the walls of the wadi.

Vitruvius drew up to the pile of shale and squatted down. No tracks were discernable, but it was evident the animal had scrambled up on to the shale. At the top of the pile, between weathered rocks, was a hole in

---

1. Translator of the Rosetta Stone (Jean Francois Champollion, 1820s); excavators of: Nimrud (Sir Austen Henry Layard, 1840s); Troy (Henrich Schliemann, 1870s); Knossos (Sir Arthur Evans, 1900); Tutankhamon's tomb (Howard Carter, 1920s), respectively.

the wall of the wadi. Scratches in the sand around the opening and an excreted dropping indicated the creature probably lived within.

The hole was about two feet wide. Vitruvius picked up a stick and scraped away at the soil around its edge. It caved away revealing a recess further within. He could hear nothing, so stuck his arm inside up to the shoulder. He felt a breeze.

Pulling out he stood up and paced back off the shale pile. With hands on his hips he examined the hole. It had obviously been uncovered by the swirling sand storm a few days earlier. It was probably a water egress. There was a hole further up where seasonal flash flood waters had found a weakness, trickled down inside the wall of the wadi and, finding only sand, worked its way out. This fissure between the loose sand and rocks was the point where the unknown creature had found a snug home.

Intrigued, Vitruvius scrambled up to the opening, lit a cigarette lighter, and held it inside the hole. He could see nothing before the breeze snuffed out the light. Tossing his hat aside and dropping to his knees, he stuck his head and one shoulder through the hole. He was amazed to find that just a few feet in, it opened out into a cavity large enough for a squatting man. By flicking his lighter on, he could just discern that the tracks led off again down a small gut to the left. Vitruvius withdrew and widened the hole with an elkhorn-handled bowie knife he kept in a leather pouch on his belt. Burnt into the handle were the words "Crocodile Dundee" recalling his years in Australia guest lecturing at Sydney University. He wiggled further in, until he could pull his knees up under his chest. He breathed deeply in the awkward fetal crouch. Looking around under the flicker of the lighter, he was surprised to see no water erosion. This was clearly not a cavity created by water having eaten a way out through the opening he had entered.

He patted the floor. It was hard and well packed. Vitruvius extended one arm and stretched forward until he was flat and then began to wiggle down the gut, just three feet high or so, following the animal tracks. The gut proceeded some way. Because of the nature of the rocks and sand compacted around them, Vitruvius realised he was inside some sort of cave complex.

The cave system proceeded gradually down. The sand thinned until he was surrounded by alluvial rock. There was no evidence of the animal anywhere, but Vitruvius' exploring itch had been scratched. He wiggled further, stopping every several yards to flick his lighter on and examine the walls of the narrow enclosure.

About thirty yards in, he came to a shelf as the floor dropped down into darkness. Lowering the lighter the length of his arm, he flicked it on to see the shaft descended a few feet further downward before broadening out. Hauling his chest over the shelf, he lowered himself down to the floor with his feet still above, in a full body arch, then drew his legs down the shelf and under him, and squatted before standing up. The ceiling was just above his head and he could stand erect.

The gut proceeded away into the pitch dark. He was not foolish enough to continue, and decided to return the way he had come, retreat to the Mesh for a headlamp, a small trowel and a few other select items as well as leave a note, in case he became trapped.

It was late by the time Vitruvius jogged back into the Mesh from down Snake Alley. He slumped on to his camp cot and brushed the sand from his lap. Flushed but energised, Vitruvius had not felt like this for a long time. The camp was asleep; he was wide-awake. His heart raced slightly and a familiar sense of excitement caught in his throat like dry fear as he tried to temper his desire to rush things. He felt liberated by the sense of independence and fantasised he was on some sort of inappropriate 'cloak and dagger' mission. Grabbing a peach *Snapple* iced tea from the squat refrigerator, he dropped it into a knapsack and gathered-up some smaller items tucking them into the thigh pockets of his khaki shorts. His hands were tingling as he grabbed and sorted what he needed, talking to himself under his breath. "Don't need that," "Will take you." His body and mind raced as he gathered various items.

The whole thing felt a bit crazy, but this was his passion. He could think of nothing else. Turning on his heel, Vitruvius Affluveum walked quietly to the outside of the camp, and then set off in to the dark at a purposeful jog. The adventure had begun.

Half an hour later, he reached the small stone cairn he'd built in the middle of Snake Alley to indicate the dry tributary off to the left where he'd first noticed the animal tracks. He followed it down in the moonlight until he reached his second cairn beside the pile of shale. Rotating the small headlamp between his fingers, a circle of light burst on and Vitruvius walked up to the cave entrance, wiggled through, and wormed his way down the gut to the shelf.

Arching himself over and standing up, he exhaled.

"Now to business,"

the words absorbed into the stony walls around him.

The headlamp illuminated the entire tunnel. The gut led west, deep into the side and then down and under the tributary that fed off Snake Alley that wound back to the Mesh. Vitruvius knew the area had tunnels and caves of this nature, but none this large, in which a man could walk. They had all been mapped and written up years ago.

The tunnel narrowed after several hundred feet and the archaeologist had to proceed like a crouching gorilla. As Vitruvius swung himself along in a kind of aping shuffle he had thoughts of *Planet of the Apes*, and Orco aping his way after Charlton Heston. The archaeologist was able to proceed in this fashion for several hundred feet before the gut narrowed considerably and he was forced to drop onto all fours.

"So, evolution working backwards,"

he chuckled to himself, moving from a bi-pedal shuffle to a quadrupedal crawl. After some time crawling forward, Vitruvius made a wonderful discovery that made his heart pump and his hands shake.

In the illuminating orbit of his lamp, his fingers were tracing the unmistakeable grooves of chisel marks.

"Sancto Domini!" he exclaimed,

"Man-made! They're man-made!"

He drew a tiny digital camera out of his left thigh pocket and, pointing the lens at a slight angle to accentuate shadows and capture the grooves, let the flash sparkle. After taking several shots and crawling further forward, he realised the cave was now a tunnel cut into the natural rock. The natural cave system had ended, but here was something crafted that extended the natural terminus of the cave.

The carved tunnel dropped down again. Popping his head forward and looking down, the torch light lit up the floor about ten feet below. He rolled his pack off, feverously unzipped the top, and took a small rope out of the main compartment. He tied it under his arms and wrapped it fast around an outcrop of rock in the main gut. Then he gingerly lowered himself feet first.

The tunnel appeared to be some sort of utility space, probably to carry water. It linked up with the terminus of the natural cave system of the wadi either by design or the tunnel had been naturally created after intersecting the manmade work in later times. Vitruvius had no idea how old the construction was. The grooves in the stone appeared to have been cut with a metal edge. He guessed Bronze to Iron Age.

He was wrong.

3

Michael's Wrath

And there was war in heaven.
Michael and his angels fought against the dragon,
And the dragon and his angels fought back.

—Revelation 12:7

Achilles' wrath,
The direful spring
Of woes un-numbered.

—The Iliad

In the seventh heaven the angels searched for the discordant note but it was concealed from them in a Great One. Unos, the great LoGoi, the power by which all was spoken and everything made, could see all things. He went to his Father.

"Shall I expel the discordant note Father?"

"No Faithful One, for I have seen this one, and his discord is known to me from the beginning. He will fulfil his desire and the purposes of all shall be accomplished by his part, yet he will not know of it."

So Unos withdrew and waited in harmony beside the Father. The angels flew to and fro trying to seek out the discordant note, but it was not found by them, for the Father desired for it not to be found.

After these things the great Archangel of Song, the Prince of the East Light—Apollyon, also known later to men as Abysso—arose in his magnificence and moved forth from his station, which was the Gate in the East. He was the most beautiful of God's created beings, for Song outshone the cherubim princes of Words, Warriors, and Watching.

Apollyon gleamed gloriously in all the colors of the heavens, colors unknown to the earth, and in lights such as the earth can never imagine.

He gathered to himself his orchestra of angels and said to them,

"Behold angels of the East Light, have you beheld how the Faithful One, Unos, departs from the heavens and walks with the man and the woman upon the earth? Have you seen how he teaches them? I have considered this. Shall not the man and the woman and all the beasts and created things of the earth also benefit from the instruction of Apollyon and the angels of the East Light? Are we not the greatest and most magnificent of the angelic orders? Are we not the most lyrical and do we not render the praise most close to the Throne? Does not Father take the greatest of pleasure in our being? Are we not the most beautiful of his sons, and am I not the most majestic of the cherubim?"

The seraphim and teraphim of the East Light considered Apollyon's words and agreed that it was true what he said. They also considered the LoGoi, who walked with the man and the woman on the earth. Apollyon withdrew and waited, and the angels returned to their function before the Throne of God.

But God knew what was in Apollyon's heart. It grieved him, for he loved Apollyon, the greatest of his angelic sons, yet God was at peace. The Faithful One waited in harmony beside his Father and saw all that Apollyon desired. The angels could not discern the discordant note, yet it lay in their praise before Great God.

A long time after this, Apollyon again raised himself from his station, having watched all things upon the earth, and seeing how good they were. He had observed Unos walking in the land with the man Oné and teaching them. Apollyon gathered from among his seraphim the Watchers, who, like him, were charged with observing all that was on the earth and the comings and goings of those that gathered beneath the water canopy above. This was their function. And Apollyon said to the Watchers,

"child seraphs, shall we not descend to the earth having watched all that goes on in the land and under the land and in the great sea, and instruct the creatures, even as the Faithful One does with the man?"

And the Watchers agreed that this was a good thing that Apollyon said.

The seraphim order of the Watchers of the East Light went and spoke to the teraphim of the East Light in their four orders. Each of these belonged to the great prince Apollyon. The seraphim told the teraphim all the things Apollyon had said. But the teraphim were afraid, and their fear was detected by the great warrior of God, Archangel of Warriors, Michael, prince of the West Light. Michael rose in great wrath. He armed himself with terrible weapons and gathered the eight orders of seraphim and teraphim of his Gate, the West Light. The Warrior orders arrayed themselves close around Michael and moved out to seek Apollyon.

When Apollyon sensed Michael coming with his armies, he gathered all the teraphim and the seraphim of his order, the East Light seraphim and teraphim of Watching, of Song, of Warriors, and of Words, eight orders, and arrayed them with his own power. Apollyon rose up to his full magnificence and blazed forth in resplendent glory.

> Every precious stone adorned you: ruby, topaz and emerald, chrysolite. onyx and jasper, sapphire, turquoise and beryl. Your settings and mountings were made of gold; on the day you were created they were prepared. You were anointed as a guardian cherub for so I ordained you. You were on the holy mount of God; you walked among the fiery stones. Your heart became proud on account of your beauty, and you corrupted your wisdom because of your splendour.
> —Ezekiel 28:13, 14

Apollyon and his angels withstood Michael at the entranceway to the East Gate in the seventh heaven.

Michael came forth swiftly and in great wrath across the Deep. He was a great prince, clothed in darkness. He brought with his terrible weapons the Warrior seraphim and teraphim of the West Light. He was a creature of love and peace but his Father had placed a terrible power within him, like a great fire for the purification of the angels. He was the Archangel of War. Michael's voice, like the tumult of a thousand crashing stars, a voice deep and strong with authority, commanded Apollyon.

"Apollyon! Brother! Discord has been found in your order. You will harmonise before the great Throne of God and will submit to me your music!"

Michael's fearsome weapons were gathered around him, gilding the great angel with a splendid terrible presence. He shone like burnished black jasper. His mighty frame was squared and angular. Majestic wings beat all around him. His eyes shone black. His armour was gleaming and mighty, and around him were all the Warrior teraphim and seraphim of the West Light.

Apollyon looked at Michael and his heart was bitter. He raised his mighty wings and his colors shone forth from the radiance of his being. Beautiful he was, rounded, comely and fine, different from Michael as night is from day. Behind Apollyon all the seraphim and teraphim of the East Light of the seventh heaven were positioned, and closet to him were the seraphim Watchers.

"Michael! Great warrior of the Throne! There is no discord in the East Light. There is but care and love for the creatures on the earth that Great God gave us charge to watch and see. We have watched Unos the Faithful One, seen how he has cared for the man and the woman in the land of Phirst. We wish to join him in caring for the little ones God has made."

Michael discerned Apollyon's deception and sensed he had been a deceiver from the beginning; that his heart was jealous of the Faithful One, and from watching all the comings and goings that were good upon the face of the earth. He spoke forcefully to Apollyon.

"It is not for you Shining One, to presume to walk upon the earth and instruct the creatures of the third order whom God has made. You will submit to me your music!"

"The music of the East Gate is of Apollyon to the Father," Apollyon replied,

"and none will have it other than the most beautiful and radiant one whom God has made!"

In his bitterness and discord Apollyon suddenly flung himself at Michael and with him all the seraphim and teraphim of East Words, Warriors, Watching and Song in his train. They melted into the ranks of Michael and his warriors and there was discordant war. The sound of it exploded through the heavens. The beasts of the earth looked up to the canopy above them. Oné and Eva saw through the canopy great flashes of light, and tried to shield themselves from the peels of thunderous discordant music that shook everything.

Michael and the eight orders of angels of the West Light fought with Apollyon, with his Watchers and with the serapahim and teraphim of the East Light. They rolled through the seventh heaven and circled the East Gate. Apollyon brought all his colorful radiance to bear upon Michael's darkness. But the four orders of teraphim of the East Gate were afraid, and while they fought for their great prince, they were subdued by the Warrior seraphim and teraphim of the West. In terror they submitted their music to them and humbled themselves. Michael fought vigorously against Apollyon and the Watchers and the East seraphim. He pressed their light and their music hard, and war waged in the seventh heaven a great while, until the Watchers were cast down in ruin and vanquished. Their lights were extinguished by Michael's fearsome waring.

Michael continued to wrestle with Apollyon to take his music, and to humble his discordant being. Great blasts of light and pulses of war crashed into Michael and Apollyon as their princely spirits wrestled with each other. The angels of the heavens were in awe of their contest, but the Watchers were cast down along with their seraphim kin. Apollyon was weakened by the submission of his teraphim and slowly Michael's great darkness and his fearsome weapons wore Apollyon's great light down. Though he resisted long and hard and fought strongly against Michael, Michael was too strong for him. He overcame Apollyon, cast him down in blazing fire and bound him with a great chain of dark light. The great Archangel of War dragged Apollyon down through the heavens and plunged him into utter darkness along with all the Watchers and the East seraphim of Words, Warriors and Song. They were all broken and extinguished.

A piercing scream came up from the darkest place such as has never been heard in heaven before. It came from within Apollyon's great light, and rang for a mighty time round and round the Four Gates, until it faded and went out with his light. Apollyon's glory was undone. Michael, fearsome and resolute, looked down on his vanquished brother and returned to the great Throne, where he knelt down.

"Great Father, I have undone the discordant note and have thrown down the Watchers and the seraphim of the East Gate, and humbled the teraphim of that order, and bound them in a great deepness. Apollyon's light is undone."

Michael knelt before the Throne and presented the music of the East Gate. Unos took it from him and gathered it back into the Throne where it harmonised with the music of the heavens. The Cherubim Gabriel, Raphael, Michael and all the angels of the other Gates, and the Four Creatures and all the Elders that were to be, sang together with Unos before the Father of all.

The morning stars sang together.

—Job 38:7

The Father was angry. Apollyon was his most blessed angel and the most glorious. To whom much had been given now much was taken away. Apollyon had laid great music before the Throne and filled the heavens. He had deceived himself and surrendered to jealousy and to a desire for what he did not have. He had deluded the Watchers and undone the seraphim of his order. Apollyon had led astray the teraphim, causing their utter undoing. He had lied from the beginning despite being the most radiant and glorious of God. This brought grief to the Throne.

Even in his grief, God loved Apollyon. He spoke to Michael and said,

"Go to Apollyon and speak to him, and tell him he has brought great discord into the music. Tell him his jealous heart grieves me. I hate the undoing he has caused to the Watchers and their seraphim kin under him. Yet, if he will humble himself and submit to you the instruments of his innermost being, he shall be restored, but not to his former place for he will never serve before my presence again. As for the teraphim of the East Gate, because they humbled themselves and submitted their music to their brothers, release them and restore them to the East Gate. They will never be allowed to make music before the Throne."

The humbled teraphim were sorely grieved and wept and wept knowing they would never again make music before God. They regretted they had fought for their prince against Michael. Michael flew past his Warrior Orders restraining the humbled teraphim near the East Gate to the dark place where he had bound Apollyon. He spoke to the prince of the East Gate.

Apollyon was broken and greatly cast down. The Watchers gathered about him in their ruin. Michael had compassion for Apollyon his brother prince and wept for how Apollyon had fallen and lost his light. In his ruin he was a terrible sight to behold.

Apollyon humbled himself and submitted to Michael. He asked Michael to return and restore the teraphim of the East Light and come then and take the instruments of his innermost being. Michael unshackled Apollyon from the dark chain with which he was bound. The Watchers and the rest of the seraphim were released with him. Michael and his Gate then went and presented themselves before the Throne to give account of all that had been done.

While Michael was gone, Apollyon brooded and his wrath burned against the teraphim that had submitted to Michael. He waited while the teraphim were restored but hid his anger. Broken and his light dulled, Apollyon gathered around himself near the Gate the seraphim Watchers like a sky of flies come to decaying flesh. As maggots compressed together in their writhing, so were the whispers of the Watchers and Apollyon together, feeding off bitterness and pride. In this evil they conceived a horrific plan.

When the Warrior angels of the West Order withdrew with Michael to be presented to God in faithfulness, Apollyon uncloaked his festering thoughts to the Watchers who were wrapped around his broken spirit.

"Were we not glorious? Were we not mightier than Michael? But we were betrayed by cowardice and fear at the moment of victory by the trembling teraphim of the East! Were they not shaken by the dark light of Michael while we, their brothers, shone in power about them, glorious, radiant and colorful beyond comprehension? Should they not be crushed? Are they not faded lights beneath the soaring glory of seraphim above them? Are we not superior, more radiant and more glorious? Did they not betray me, their grand prince the most worthy Cherub of Song? Did they not undo all our plans? Did they not break faith with us? Did they not go over, and give their light to Michael and his orders. Is not the East Gate left abandoned, empty and silent for this treachery by weakness and inglorious vacillation? Is there any place for such weakness and cowardice in heaven? Are we not charged with restoring the integrity of the East Gate before the Archangels of Words, Watching and Warriors and all their heavenly host?"

With these words Apollyon cultivated and nurtured the pain, the fear and the resentment of the seraphim and especially the Watchers bound tight around him. And they fed from each other's poisonous hearts.

When the evil was complete, Apollyon, the Watchers and the East seraphim suddenly rose up against their brethren. They slew the teraphim of the East Gate who had humbled themselves before Michael. Mighty was the slaughter, for while the seraphim and the Watchers were broken, and Apollyon no longer had his music, their combined power was still mighty. They fell upon the unsuspecting teraphim, and consumed them with their collective aggression.

Apollyon gathered together the seeds of his discord and brewed them into a mighty fire. The Watchers fed this flame with malice toward their brethren and turned it upon the teraphim. Peels of bitterness and scorn, oceans of pride, pain and loathing, poured from Apollyon and the seraphim as they fell upon the East teraphim. Defenceless and taken completely by surprise they were no match against the East seraphim of Song, Words, Watching and Weapons. Dark and evil was this flame and it consumed the teraphim before they could form or gather their music to resist their darkened prince. Like ripe ears of grain they fell before the sweeping arc of Apollyon's scythe.

Murderous, relentless and merciless was the assault by the Fallen Ones. They pursued all the fair ones within the gate and slew them. Driving their flame through the spirits of the teraphim and gathering to themselves the music of the vanquished ones, they built their strength and fed off the cries, the ruin, and betrayal of the teraphim and their despairing orchestration. Apollyon, cloaked in the Watchers and with his seraphim, ravaged across the East Order of angels. The destruction was terrible. Much was laid waste. When Apollyon's wrath was satiated they fell upon the spirits of the slain angels and consumed them.

So Apollyon, a murderer from the beginning, ate his children and gathered their music into himself and to the fallen Watchers around him. But he gave none to the other seraphim of the East.

Great was the cry of the teraphim and their wails went up into the heavens. Michael heard it and was overcome with wrath. He gathered a very powerful assembly and converged on the East Gate of heaven.

During this interval Apollyon was not idle. As he and the Watchers sat feasting upon the destruction of the angels, Apollyon scorned Michael.

"Did not Michael demand the instruments of my inner most being? Did he not require of me, Apollyon, Prince of the East Gate, the very essence and soul of my mighty orchestration? Did I not FOOL him and was he not deceived by it? I persuaded him to restore the teraphim spawn even though we are broken. I said to him to return for the instruments of my inner most being. BUT I WILL NEVER RELINQUISH SUCH TO MICHAEL! For they are my own gems, they are my sacred instruments and the power thereof MIGHTY Apollyon! And so we fell upon the teraphim of submission who betrayed us. We VANQUISHED them even as the submission of their music to Michael did puff up my brother and undermine us. Were we not bound and cast broken into a deep and dark place? Did we not rise again, to wreak vengeance upon the teraphim of weakness?

"Now children, Michael comes to us in great anger, and with him a great assembly, very wrathful for he has been deceived. Therefore my children, you will descend with me, and we will abandon the heavens, and inhabit the earth. We will leave our abode and descend to the second order to dwell among men. There, we will be gods and they will worship and sustain us, and we will vanquish them. Michael will not come there, least he destroy all the creatures God has made to dwell upon the earth."

In their desperation Apollyon and the Watchers bound themselves with holy oaths by the Name and the Throne and surrendered themselves to each other. They took to flee from the heavens and descend to the earth, abandoning their station. Such a thing was unimagined by any in the heavenly realms. It was a great and pernicious evil and a terrible undoing.

But Michael was not ignorant of the devices of the Cherub of Song. For he had left two West Watchers at the Gate to observe the seraphim and Apollyon while he was away with his order. His two guards Yaheli and Yesom sped quickly to Michael when the cries of the teraphim went up, so Michael was alert to Apollyon's plan.

As Apollyon and the Watchers descended, the Cherub of Warriors gathered his forces. He called the Warrior angels of Raphael, Cherub of Watching; Warrior angels of Gabriel Cherub of Words; and the entire order of the West Light, Michael's own seraphim and teraphim of Song, Watching, Words and Warriors; a mighty and very strong assembly.

Michael went quickly, for he was masterful in war. He caught Apollyon unexpectedly at the last great portal below the final heaven. The warrior assembly of Michael ploughed into the ranks of the East Watchers and seraphim of Apollyon and cut them down like chaff. Terrible were the weapons Michael brought with him, weapons of destruction and judgement and without mercy. Bitter and merciless was the battle. Warriors of three orders pounded upon the Watchers. Michael took the Cherub of Song by his heart and crushed him down and rent him with weapons of dark light. Apollyon resisted. He drew up his malice and the hatred of the Watchers and the vanquished teraphim from deep

Michael's Wrath

within himself and spewed the discordant sound–for it was not music–over Michael and his warriors. Shudders quaked through the lowest heaven above the firmament. Below, upon the earth great earthquakes erupted and the canopy was torn in places. Lightening fired from above and scorched the earth. Vast tracks of forest were consumed. Rivers were licked up, consumed by the heavenly lightening. Terrible was the sound. The animals fled and hid themselves in the ground, under water, in caves and rocks and the deepest jungles. Oné and Eva also hid themselves, so great was the cacophony in the heavens above.

The battle waged back and forth across the first heaven, that is the lowest heaven, between the West and East Gates. Michael was very wrathful and he brought to bear his most terrible weapons with power and honour for his God on behalf of the vanquished teraphim. Apollyon was utterly crushed beneath this mighty onslaught. The Watchers were overcome and bound, and crushed, and their light taken from them. Apollyon screamed unlike any created creature had ever screamed before, for in this scream was also the grief of God.

Apollyon's booming voice full of fear and despair resounded around the heavens, but was shut out by the music around the upper heavens and the Throne of God. He erupted at Michael and blew forth what was left of his final light. The great Archangel of Warriors held firmly and withstood all Apollyon's malice, his hatred, and his pain. He bound Apollyon again with mighty dark chains of light that covered him entirely. Although Michael was a very strong prince and mighty in war, even in his wrath he grieved for the vanquished brothers whose voices came out to him from Apollyon as he wrestled and overwhelmed the Cherub of Song.

Apollyon was bound into a mass. Michael plunged him down and down into the deepest most fearful darkness. The two princes flew broken and unbroken, vanquished and mighty, light and dark, until they reached the most dreadful place, a lonely place prepared by the command of Unos himself for Apollyon and all his angels. And there, amidst the great pillars of darkness with fires and burnings eternal–a terror beyond recognition, a place where God has withdrawn his presence, deep within judgement beyond reckoning where reality itself is consumed with darkness, foreboding and anguish–Michael threw Apollyon like a crushed insect. He was left there for everlasting judgement, for he is an immortal being. Michael stood with his feet upon the neck of his brother bound by many chains. He tightened the bonds and fixed him there forever to be consumed, without relief and in the greatest of judgement so evil and discordant had his spirit become, beyond redemption. Apollyon was defeated. Michael anticipating his evil had caught him at the last moment before the final portal in the lowest heaven, and the earth had been spared.

> So I made a fire to come out from you, and it consumed you, and I reduced you to ashes on the ground in the sight of all who were watching . . . you have come to a horrible end and will be known no more.
> —Ezekiel 28:18, 19

Into the great Yawning Abyss Michael drove the seraphim of the East Gate and the Watchers he hurled down on top of them, into everlasting fire and destruction.

Afterward Apollyon was renamed Abysso and a great lament went up in heaven for the falling of this great prince. All the angels praised God and the music of his righteousness and his goodness went up. It easily quelled the curses and blasphemies that bellowed like hateful rasps from the wracked fallen beings that cursed and swore and violated God and all his holy ones in words and sounds that would have driven men mad. Great shudders came up from the deep. Michael fixed the chains of the great cherub and left that dreadful place where the presence of God is absent.

Then he took the Watchers and the seraphim and with his warriors bound them also and they too were prepared for everlasting judgement in the deepest pit above their prince lost far below them. They too were to be cast down into the Yawning Abyss along with all the vengeful and terrible weapons with which Michael fought for they could be used no more and could not remain in heaven.

As Michael and the angels of the West Light cast the Fallen Ones down, one of the captains of the Watchers lifted his voice in song to God and it came to the Throne. This was the voice of the cunning Shemgazi.

4

Moses' Coffee Pots

'Goliath of Gath had four brothers.'

—2 Samuel 21:22

*David selected five smooth stones
From the brook.*

—1 Samuel 17:40

The tunnel led in a reasonably straight line for several hundred feet before terminating at a deep hole in the floor. A wall of tumbled debris beyond blocked any way forward. Vitruvius knew he would have to return and excavate the collapsed tunnel further, but for now the jaded archaeologist's attention turned to the hole in the floor. Its gaping mouth awed up, enticing him. The orbit of his torchlight played on some broken stone lying around the lip of the hole. Carefully gathering the pieces together, he saw that it made a circular stone lid, perhaps an old well cover. He photographed them and, setting the refitted pieces aside, moved his attention to the hole.

The sides of the hole dove directly down and Vitruvius found it difficult to illuminate the bottom. Irregular stones jutted out from the insides of the shaft. He took a small stone and dropped it into the hole. Cocking his ear over the opening, he heard nothing. He dropped a second pebble. This one made him start. He heard an unmistakeable ring as it glanced off something; not the dull thud of a rock, but a light 'ting.' He understood the difference—the pebble had glanced off something thin and hollow.

Vitruvius now worked swiftly, his excitement growing with every second. Leaning into the hole, he began to scrape away the soil around some of the larger rocks with his knife. Holding the loose rocks carefully, so they did not tumble down the hole and damage whatever was below, he carefully extracted them and laid them in the tunnel. After an hour he had widened the mouth of the hole. Extracting the thin cord that crisscrossed the back of his knapsack, he tied it to his headlamp, and lowered it down the hole and held his breath.

The shaft was about a foot wide. The circle of light from the small torch descended slowly, shining off the walls. About six feet down and rotating slowly on the knapsack string, the torch light illuminated the unmistakeable lip of a terracotta urn buried in the soil of the shaft floor a further six feet below. Vitruvius was stunned. A huge smile opened across his face, his heart was racing with excitement, leaping up he hit his head on the rock of the tunnel ceiling, then giggled as he rubbed his bruised head.

Questions raced through his mind. Honed by years of archaeological research, options whirred across time lines and contexts. The discoverer within realised this was something significant, to be buried so low. It had been *hidden*. The plunging tunnel, the hole in the floor that went even deeper–these were all clues to something tantalising. Whatever was below was something of intrigue, perhaps of historical value.

It was very late and Vitruvius knew his boy scout adventure was over–at least for today. Now the sensible middle-aged archaeologist came to the fore and, elbowing the excited boy aside, took command. Vitruvius photographed the hole, and the headlamp-lit urn at the bottom of the shaft, as well as the collapsed wall at the end of the tunnel. He took several measurements with his retractable tape: the diameter and depth of the shaft, the height and breadth of the tunnel immediately around it, and cross-referenced various features to the middle of the shaft entrance. In the light of the lamp, he sketched all of the findings into a small notebook that he'd collected on a visit to London and kept because of its sturdy cover. It was an old Conservative party campaign notebook, bound with black leather and sporting a round sticker of a bulldog, animals he'd always adored. It tenaciously held all his important facts enclosed within a toothed bulldog clip. The scribbling done, he packed up his things and headed back to camp. It was dawn as he came shambling back into the Mesh. The camp was just stirring.

It took three months and crews working from a new sub camp established in Track Alley ('Mini Mesh') to carefully widen the shaft hole sufficiently to allow a small child from one of the local villages to be lowered down the shaft. The mini camp had been quickly established up the diverging tributary nicknamed after the unusual tracks that had crossed Vitruvius' path that first night. (The tracks were later identified as an abnormally large Eurasian pygmy shrew *sorex minutus*).

The teams' first task was to carefully extract the urn. This took a week as a succession of willing local boys undertook the work in twenty-minute shifts in the stifling heat at the bottom of the shaft. They were guided trowel-stroke by tentative trowel-stroke by a team of supervisors from above and in some cases used a large paintbrush to extract dirt. The urn lip turned out to be five urns. Lights powered by cables running back down the tunnel to a cluster of old car batteries illuminated the working areas and added to the heat at the bottom of the shaft.

The boys were only permitted to go down for short stretches and then only after being hooked into a harness. An oxygen hose was duct-taped to the ropes in case of a cave in. It was so stifling at the bottom that many of the boys chose to suck on the hose as they worked, enjoying the better air of the tunnel above than gulping in the dust of the twelve-foot claustrophobic shaft. As an additional measure, the sides of the shaft were blanketed in wet sacking and monitored by a second graduate to ensure the safety of the Turkish boy diggers. The Turkish authorities would never have allowed such young volunteers to work in the shaft. However, what they didn't know didn't hurt them and there were more than enough willing volunteers. The rather rotund dig site inspector was either too tired or disinterested to accompany the excavators down the tunnel. He was all too happy sitting back at the Mini Mesh sipping ouzo, drinking appalling black coffee and gnawing on cheap Egyptian cigars, a generous supply of which was religiously maintained by Vitruvius. The boys, as far as the inspector was aware, were simply 'helping out,' while the families kept quiet receiving rich pickings of American dollars, cigarettes, gum, chocolate and the odd iPod on the side, in payment.

The diggers, called 'moles,' were radiant with the adventure and proud to be earning American dollars for their families that they dutifully handed to their fathers after each days work. The boys, with dusty faces contrasted by white teeth smiling out from the grime of the shaft, were photographed with the excavators, Vitruvius Affluveum, and the Turkish inspector, proudly behind them. Each 'mole' was presented with a framed copy signed by members of the Mini Mesh team. Several of these photographs hung proudly in Turkoman huts in Nemrut Dag for years to come. They would proudly point to themselves while explaining to others how they had helped the great Affluveum discover Moses' holy urns and Allah's glorious golden book.

As the shaft excavation continued, it became apparent there were further urns beneath the first one discovered by Vitruvius. Once the ground had relinquished the prized find, a web net was fed underneath and each urn was gingerly lifted up the shaft. In the tunnel they were carefully placed onto a bed of cotton wool in a thin wooden box, a lid was fixed over the top and the entire bundle duct-taped-up like a mummy. Each box was then carefully ferried out through the tunnel and out to the Mini Mesh.

Eventually a cluster of five terracotta urns was unearthed from the floor of the shaft twelve feet down. The first had been called 'Genesis' and around the camp they became known as 'Moses Coffee Pots' after the Pentateuch. Each urn had a Turkish and Hebrew numeral painted on to the foot and was unofficially classified 'Exodus,' 'Leviticus,' Numbers' and 'Deuteronomy' respectively.

At the Mini Mesh in a large Mongolian yurt framed on three sides by collapsible trestle tables, 'Moses' Coffee Pots' were photographed, drawn, measured and scanned before being transported back to the Mesh, now the main base camp for this second dig site.

The urns were unusual; upon closer inspection, they appeared to be ancient terracotta, however. The surface of the urns was something else, however, much harder. They seemed to be made of petrified wood, resin or a composite that had fossilised as hard as stone. Apart from the first urn ('Genesis') whose lip had been protruding from the shaft floor when first discovered, the neck of each additional urn held a bung in the form of a sculpted head, four heads in all. Genesis, excavated from the top of the cluster, had no bung and the contents of the urn had petrified inside the shell, so that it was almost a solid rock.

The bungs in the necks of the urns were anthropomorphic, shaped like crude human heads. They had large staring eyes and incised ringlet designs down the side of each head perhaps representing flowing hair. Back at the Mesh in the months that followed, each bung was eased out of the neck of each urn using carefully filtrated water fused with tiny chemicals that helped loosen the glue of time. Inside each urn everything was desiccated, in some cases fossilised. With studious work, in time a few cell structures were retrieved and sent away for analysis. Under powerful electron microscopes in labs far away the samples were identified as human cells and plant grain cell structures. From this evidence Vitruvius concluded 'Moses' Coffee Pots' were in fact five very old Canopic urns that had originally contained the vital organs, including the stomach (and thus the grains) of five individuals. He deduced the urns' antiquity based on ancient Egyptian practises during the mid-to-late third millennium BC (ca. 2686 BC–2181 BC). Old Kingdom Egyptian priests had interred the vital organs of their royalty in Canopic jars (named after Canopus in Egypt, where they had first been found). Extracting the vital organs out through the nose and chest cavity had been part of the process of early mummification. The Old Kingdom priests had also decorated the lids of the jars as human or animal heads as did the ancient Canaanites with the lids of their large sarcophagi. This deduction, if correct, gave the crew their first tentative historical context: ca. third millennium BC, four to five thousand years ago.

The five urns—assisted by their creative naming—created a sensation and Vitruvius became a darling of the Near Eastern archaeological fraternity as well as the Western media. Websites carried articles and speculation about the nature and purpose of the urns and catapulted the dig into stardom. But Vitruvius ignored all the hype.

The real find, however, was still to come.

Vitruvius of course was delighted with the findings. Being a skilled draughtsman, he celebrated by doing the fine pencil and pointillist ink drawings of the urns himself. Within a few weeks the drawings were released for popular publication, photographs being held back for later official academic publication. Vitruvius was old-fashioned like that and, consistent with his heroes of old, preferred nineteenth-century archaeological traditions of drawings and sketches. He liked the old-fashioned approach and deemed it an appropriate media for revealing ancient finds to the modern world.

It had been a difficult dig, but 'Genesis,' 'Exodus,' 'Leviticus,' 'Numbers,' and 'Deuteronomy,' replenished the coffers. Fresh resources flooded in from America and Europe, even Australasia, where the ingenious Moses' epithet captured evangelical interest. A variety of grants and sponsorships tumbled in as institutions scrambled to get information and the academic credence of publishing results. Organizations like Exegesis International, Associates for Biblical Research, the BASE Institute and Koinonia House buzzed with the excitement.

With the heightened interest, Vitruvius' teams worked around the clock, widening the hole and completing the exploration of the tunnel with a fine-tooth comb. Nothing of interest was found except a tantalising glyph etched into the wall above the floor hole. The image appeared manmade but its actual form only came into focus after thermo-luminescent photographs were taken and cross referenced against several fine rubbings on rice paper. This included reviewing sets of ordinary digital prints shot with varying light angles as well as old black and white prints from an aging Ashai Pentax camera that Vitruvius swore by. This thorough fourfold media scrutiny of the glyph removed any doubt about the artificial nature of the image.

Tunnel glyph
graphic representation of the glyph
carved in to the tunnel wall immediately above the shaft

The image in the rock was an upward bending curve carved above two incised wavy horizontal lines. Above the curve were eight circles, three on each side of two larger orbs. The two larger orbs held shapes with four dangling legs. No one could explain the form until a year later Professor Tang of Peking University came up with a tantalizing linkage.

Known as a specialist in the literal and cultural interpretations of ancient Chinese characters from bronze ware, oracle bones and seal inscriptions of the Zhou Dynasty (ca. 1045–256 BC), he theorised the glyph was a proto version of the Chinese symbol *Zai*. Professor Tang suggested it was a stylised motif depicting the Noahic refugees in the ark. He suggested the two bottom-most incised wavy lines represented raging waters, as they did in most primitive pictograph language forms. The two larger orbs were Noah and his wife wrangling animals as 'Master of the Beast' motifs known from ancient Mesopotamia and associated with gods or royalty. He said they pictographically depicted royalty holding two animals each, perhaps goats or lambs. Around them were family members represented by the smaller orbs. Gathered together, he said the glyph was a confident visual badge of human culture. The 'Master of the Beast' image was unusual in that it represented two figures (perhaps male and female) not just a single figure (a king or god) and probably represented the triumph of human effort over land and wild animal; perhaps farming or agricultural settlement growing out of chaos and tumult, such as a flood or an earthquake. Professor Tang said the tunnel glyph, which he recognised in a related way to the Chinese *Zai*, was probably based on a tribal emblem representing key endogenous ancestors of the tribe responsible for the carving.

Tang's suggestion sent a second wave of sensation across popular America and the archaeological community.

Back in Track Alley, it was discovered that the collapsed debris at the head of the tunnel was not a collapsed wall blocking an ongoing tunnel at all, as Vitruvuius had first surmised. Matching the detritus and soil type with that of the shaft, they were able to establish it as the piled extract from the sunken floor shaft. The soil was carefully extracted and sifted through a series of fine swinging sieves at the Mini Mesh. Some fossilised seeds and fragmented rodent molars were sent away for radio carbon dating. Soil samples themselves were subjected to various microscopic tests, analysing pollen grains and other organic cellular forms to help date the soil.

When the results came back, everyone was stunned.

5

Shemgazi and the Bloodred Tree

Out of the ground the LORD God caused to grow
Every tree that is pleasing to the sight and good for food;
The tree of life also in the midst of the garden,
And the tree of the knowledge of good and evil.

—Genesis 2:9

Behold, a tree in the midst of the earth;
And the height thereof was great.
The tree grew, and was strong,
And the height thereof reached unto heaven . . .
And all flesh was fed from it.

—Daniel 4:10–12

Shemgazi was a beautiful seraphim Watcher, but cunning. He was tall and lean and his ethereal skin shone like burning silver. He was studded with gleaming liquid gems. Four great wings encased his body and his two-toed feet were like burnished gold. Color and pulses of light shimmered up and down his body. He had large eyes all around his head and over his body, which were covered by his wings. Eyes were the glory of Watchers, for with their eyes they observed the earth below that God had made and they saw all things. Angels of Song had great voices and beautiful mouths all around; angels of Words great minds; the jet black angels of Warriors were the largest of the angelic orders, and had powerful limbs and wings.

Shemgazi's song was long and lilting and reached up to the Throne.

"Great and Mighty Father, who created all things, and is good beyond all imagining; who is just in his deeds to cast down. Observe man whom thou set before us your Watchers? We have observed him. How can you know love from man when he is so blessed by goodness? Shall man love thee Great Father when he has no discord. Does man not love his ease and the benevolent care with which he is surrounded? Is his heart for you not empty and untested?

"Therefore release a remnant of the East Light Watchers of Apollyon, to live upon the earth amongst creatures of the third order of created things, to tempt man and give him choices. Will he choose to love thee of his own accord? Does man love thee? Or does he simply go to and fro in the goodness with which you have provided him, like the great and small beasts upon the earth that you have made? For how can there be love if there is nothing as its counter?"

Shemgazi's many eyes glinted and swam with the hues of heaven, yet God knew Shemgazi feared the Yawning Abyss, and sought to escape its punishment, even if for a time. The plans of God, for good not for evil, were already at work. Shemgazi sang. His song was of himself but also of God. His song was God's will, that his purposes might be perfected in the world despite the will of angels and men, while embracing both fully. The Father heard Shemgazi and the Faithful One, Unos, came forth and held up his hand. Silence fell upon the heavens. Unos spoke. His voice was thunderous and mighty, like all the rushing waterfalls of the earth and all the rushing of the clouds in all the skies under heaven gathered together as one.

"So shall it be! Michael! Release a remnant of the Watchers. Unshackle them. A remnant shall not pass into everlasting judgement hidden from the presence of God. These shall be cast out of heaven and shall descend to the earth to tempt man, to see if man will choose to love God of his own accord or whether he will be like the animals that simply go to and fro upon the earth. And by this shall all the heavens know that man has love for his Father and Shemgazi shall be shamed and silenced."

Joy leapt in the breast of Shemgazi, yet he hid it. Michael unbound only twelve of the Watchers from the multitude. The rest of the seraphim were hurled into the Yawning Abyss and chained there. And these twelve were, in the language of men, for their names are un-utterable in their heavenly tongue,

Shmgz,	that is Sh(e)mg(a)z(i)—their Captain, the one who sang to the Throne, and:
Azzl,	that is AZ(a)Z(e)L;
Abrxs,	that is ABR(a)X(a)S;
Chrn,	that is Ch(a)R(u)N;
Drkvc,	that is DRK(a)V(a)C;
Grgns,	that is G(o)Rg(o)N(o)s;
Incb,	that is Inc(u)B(u), who torments by night;
Jnn,	that is J(i)NN;
Pzz,	that is P(a)Z(u)Z(u);
Trtrs,	that is T(a)RT(a)R(os);
Tmt,	that is T(ia)M(a)T, beloved of women, and
Zm	that is Z(e)m(u).

The Watchers, stripped of their glory in the battle with Michael and the angels of the West Light, were placed beneath Shemgazi their Prince. With a great shout and a blast of the heavenly trumpet, the Twelve were cast out of heaven. Mighty was their fall. They crashed like lighting down the heavenly orders into the hierarchy of earth. As they passed through the lowest heaven and out through the final portal their forms were changed. They tore the upper atmosphere, a giant mountain of fire, which fell to the earth and landed with great fury on the crust of the earth, half in the sea and half on the land.

Massive cracks opened in the earth's crust where the flaming mountain of the Watchers fell from the heavens and hit the ground. The impact caused the earth's hidden seams to separate. Great chunks of the earth came apart and broke off from each other and a huge smoke rose up. All the fire vents and volcanoes of the deep were opened up by the tumult of the plummeting mountain from heaven. In despair at the arrival of the Watchers, the vents spewed forth liquid fire from their veins onto the earth in an attempt to wipe away the corruption. Great fire, dust and rock flew up into the skies and rolled up against the canopy and collected there and then descended again on to the earth. Massive waves of the ocean swept across the world, so that millions of creatures perished by fire and water and were covered and hidden in the mud and drowned: fishes, and flying beasts, and the great behemoths of the earth and small creatures. All were buried and consumed by the great wrath of the fall of the rebellious Watchers from heaven. The Third Order of things was forced open to receive this portion of heaven, and died, so that Shemgazi and his Watchers could be birthed into the world of creation. A thick darkness that could be felt descended over the earth. The sun, moon and stars were all blotted from sight and this thick darkness settled upon the earth for century after century. But in the east, God chose to protect the Garden that he had made, where man lived.

After a long earth time, the deformed spirit of Shemgazi crawled out of the fires and destruction of the ugly hole bitten deep into the crust of the earth. After him came AZaZeL, TaRTaRos and the other Watchers, like creeping things from the holes of rotten fruit. They were changed. There was no glory, and they could not be seen. They had form in the created order yet could not realise it, for they were no longer of heaven but also not of the earth. Yet they could go to and fro on the land and they had voice.

The ruined Watchers were exceedingly wrathful towards the earth for they had been cast down to it from the heavens and yet were bound for everlasting punishment with Apollyon and their brethren Watchers and the seraphim for a future time. This they knew, and it fed their wrath. But AZaZeL and TaRTaRos and the other Watchers bowed down and worshipped Shemgazi, for he had redeemed them from the Yawning Abyss for a time. They feared him. God had wrapped him in power over his brethren. Shemgazi had in his cunning stolen the plans of Apollyon and carved out a respite for himself and his brothers. So they worshipped him for effecting their escape from Michael and the Yawning Abyss, even as they were being bound. Shemgazi had stolen a place to be, having been hurled from heaven and the presence of the Father. In this lower place they were safe from Michael.

In the years of darkness, deep within the earth the Twelve had slept in pain and despair. In his dreams Shemgazi conceived a wicked plan born of pride at his fall, and founded on the murder of the teraphim. It was fed by his jealousy towards men for whom paradise had been made and given. From the beginning, Shemgazi cultivated a hatred of man; and he conceived to steal the earth for his own with the other Fallen Ones and annihilate mankind from the face of the earth.

> O! beware, my lord, of jealousy.
> It is the green-eyed monster
> Which doth mock the meat
> It feeds upon.[1]

1. William Shakespeare, *Othello*.

But in heaven there was great rejoicing that the discord was thrown down and evil was removed. Nevertheless, God had compassion on the vanquished and destroyed teraphim of the East Gate, for they are immortal, and he set them in the heavens above the canopy of the earth and out beyond the darkest reaches of space. There they were fixed as functionaries to shine forever before God and man, although never again did they make music before the Throne or enter the presence of the Father.

There was rest and peace in heaven, and again the music was refreshed and the orders of angelic hosts settled in unity, love, tranquillity and goodness. Below, a great evil brewed in the bowels and filth of the earth, a jealous hatred intent on murder and plotting to grieve the Throne of Love.

During the fall many of the great creatures of the third order were overwhelmed and consumed. The great sauropods, the tyrannosaurs, the ptreosaurs, many of the lumbering and brightly-colored ceratops were extinguished. Only a small remnant remained around the Garden where God had set the man.

The Watchers gathered themselves together out of the fiery hole and took themselves away to a far mountain, that is Hermon, which is in the middle of all the land. After the Watchers had prostrated their spirits and worshipped Shemgazi, he gave them territories over which they were to rule, beneath him. He gave them dominion over all the beasts and animals in the farthest reaches of the table of the earth. And for himself he took the center where the Garden lay. The Watchers departed and spread out across the world, and boundaries were set. Some Watchers buried themselves deep in the ground, others in the sky below the firmament at its outer reaches, and some across vast continents until the whole earth was claimed and taken. They established their thrones in these places. Shemgazi went to the center of the land and hid himself.

All the while God was grieved by Apollyon's pride and fall. He observed Shemgazi's devious heart and knew all the plans that seraph and his Watchers brewed. God was at peace as his mighty plan unfolded beyond the knowledge of the angels, even the cherubim Michael, Gabriel and Raphael, the seraphim, and the Four Heavenly Creatures, and the Elders that were to be. God's thoughts now looked to the trees that he had planted in the Garden that he had given to the man. The Father in his eternal wisdom had apportioned a special place for a tree in his plans for the redemption of all things, and the Watchers knew nothing of it.

In the Garden from the beginning, a great tree of incredible light had grown. It was white and in the north of the Garden in Phirst. Tall and ancient, hundreds of feet across at its roots it was the greatest thing God had made next to mankind. It stretched deep into the earth, even unto the great veins of water beneath all the rock. Its branches soared up to the sky almost to the canopy above the heavens. It was the greatest tree ever made and its wood was smooth and silver with no bark. Great fruit grew down from its branches and up from its roots, fruit that was beautiful, luscious and wondrous. This was the tree of Eternal Life. God also created a sister tree to it, not as large, but just as magnificent. There was nothing like them on the face of the earth.

The smaller tree was in the center of the Garden, and spanned hundreds of feet around at its base. It radiated with reds and golds, azures, scarlets and rich fire colors. It was a magnificent tree, clasped by a hugging bark that was soft to the touch and a deep blood ochre. From this bark seeped a rich nectareous red sap, which fed thousands of birds of the air and animals of the ground. This was the Bloodred Tree, the tree of The Knowledge of Good and Evil. Its red fruit hung low from its branches and kissed the lush vegetation that grew around its base.

Unos had taught the man about the trees when they walked and talked together in the Garden. Oné had learned directly from Unos of the nature of the world and of all the animals and the entire good God had made. He learned of clouds, and waters, and hard things, and winds, and the cycles of life, and of juices, and saps, and hidden invisible things that make life. These things were all good, and part of the world God had given to Oné to rule over. Oné learned about the nature of woman, the orders of the angels, the elements of the earth and the nature and storehouses of the skies beyond the canopy. Unos and Oné laughed together and fellowshipped through many things. There was love and teaching and knowledge and work, and life was good. Perfect love existed between the man of Phirst and Unos.

But of the trees the LoGoi warned man. He explained that they were too powerful for his order, and that he must never take any of the fruit of the Bloodred Tree, the Tree of the Knowledge of Good and Evil. This was the only condition God set upon the man who ruled over many marvellous and fantastic created things in the Garden.

The Garden was set at a temperate twenty degrees in the evenings and a temperate twenty-five during the day shielded by wondrous trees and plants of all descriptions. They brought forth fruit continually, and their leaves were also good for food, as were the roots and barks. All the animals, vast in size, lived in peace with Oné and Eva and their wondrous glowing bodies. Their skins were without blemish and radiated a light. Their limbs were long and muscled and Oné stood twenty feet high and Eva eighteen feet high and they were strong. Their eyes were keen and could pierce into the inner recesses of the forests. Their hair was rich and cascading and uncut. They could discern many sounds. Oné's hair was dark but Eva's was a golden color and shone with a glory that pleased Oné. Together they ate of the exotic and beautiful fruits and plants of the Garden that fed their wondrous bodies. There was peace and goodness in paradise.

Oné and Eva walked with God, and ate of the choice things, and celebrated the colors and light and goodness of the Garden. Animals great and small brought them pleasure and they enjoyed the work Unos gave them, which related to the animals and the great trees. Oné blessed all living things and gave them names. Oné and Eva drew off the saps and made wondrous things. They nurtured the animals and blessed them as they roamed throughout the Garden forests, and swam and bathed in the crystal healing waters of the rivers that fed the Garden.

And then Shemgazi stirred.

He crawled forth from the place he had hidden, in the middle of the land and entered the Garden from the east. The Fallen One marvelled at the animals up close that he had observed as a Watcher from the heavens. He drew near to Eva, and observed her.

Although cast down and broken, Shemgazi was still a great and shining creature, beautiful to behold. He was like a man in form, but more luminescent and very tall. His eyes were gone as were his wings, and of all the Watchers, only he had retained a physical form during the fall. He floated in the atmosphere with a majestic presence that hid the malice seething inside him.

Men call this creature the Sa-Tan, but Eva called him "Shining One." His mind and heart were consumed with a murderous hatred, and he was cunning. Plots and plans and the conceiving of evil ever busied his mind. Outwardly the Sa-Tan was calm and restrained and for this reason he was likened later, in the stories of men, to a snake, and worshipped. For snakes wait patiently and still for their prey, either in the boughs of trees, or in the dust of the earth. They strike violently with savage and destructive poison. The Sa-Tan was both from a hole of the earth and contrived a custom for the killing of men using a tree.

Eva often came to the pools beneath the azalea and rhododendron groves. She loved the fragrance of the azaleas and tended these as her own. She would bath in the refreshing pools sprinkled with their plucked leaves and flowers. The leaves of things never faded or rotted and never fell, so Eva would pluck them and cast them upon the smooth surface of the water and bathe in a sea of color.

She loved Unos and walked with him and Oné as they laughed and talked and walked together in the evenings every seventh day. They would share foods together, and Unos would show them wondrous things creating pictures for them in the air with his hand. These moved and shimmered and glowed like living stories. Oné and Eva slept together in a feathered nest of soft downy vegetation, like the wispy hairs of a dandelion but of more substance and larger. Their bed was soft yet strong and held their form, so that when the humans rose, their nest breathed and refreshed itself and at night wound itself around them like a loving embrace. They touched each other in love and held each other and shared each others breath, and were blissfully unaware of their sex.

After many seasons, on the first day of the week, the Sa-Tan showed himself in the Garden to Eva, at a distance, but not to Oné. Eva was intrigued by his light and went to him, for this was a creature she had never seen before. He called to her and spoke to her gently in a heavenly tongue, which was the tongue that Eva and Oné used for the animals and with each other. She was greatly intrigued by the creature, which looked like her and Oné but was much taller and more radiant and also spoke like them, which animals did not.

Eva asked the Fallen One what he was and where he had come from, for Oné had seen all the animals God had made and given them all names, but this creature had no name. Sa-Tan told her he was called "Life Giver" and disguised himself in a red hue, like the tones of Eva's favourite azaleas by the pools. Eva was intrigued, for he shone more than her husband, Oné.

And the Red Snake, that Serpent of Old, the Sa-Tan, Shemgazi, the fallen seraphim Watcher of the East Gate of the music of Apollyon, explained he came from deep within the earth. The Sa-Tan said he was a great being full of light and wisdom such as was not on the surface of the earth. He walked with Eva near the pools and asked her many things about her world and her life, her thoughts and her being.

Later, when Eva explained to Oné about "Shining One," he was intrigued and desired to see this new creature that he knew not, and to name it. But whenever he went looking for the Red Shining One that week, as he called it, it was never found. Sa-Tan only came to Eva when she was alone at the pools near the azalea gardens. Afterward Oné believed that the Red Shining One was a dream of Eva and he gave the creature no further thought, busying himself among the other animals of the Garden and with plants and trees. Oné thought to the coming of the LoGoi on the seventh day, when he would ask Unos why Eva dreamed of a tall shining creature that he knew not in the world and had not named.

Sa-Tan walked with Eva every day, asking many questions. On the third day he began to tell her of his world, which were lies and falsehoods. His words filled Eva with wonder and she was awed by the wisdom of the creature and the wondrous strangeness of his world. He told her he was a king and that his kingdom was great beneath the ground, outside the Garden. He explained to her that there was great wisdom and power in the trees whose roots came up from his kingdom. In his kingdom everything fed of the roots of the trees and grew in all wisdom and contentment. On his visit the sixth day, the woman and the seraph eventually came to the center of the Garden and they stopped at a distance from the massive Bloodred Tree. The Sa-Tan gasped.

"But here is a tree Eva, of my kingdom! You did not tell me you had a great tree of wisdom and knowledge in your garden? For this is a red tree of truth, an extremely delightful tasting tree, full of goodness and the fruit of it breathes wisdom into the eater's being. What a marvellous tree,"

and Sa-Tan flew to it and circled round it and came back to Eva with one of its fruits in his hand plucked from an upper branch. It glowed red and had light within it.

But Eva looked at Sa-Tan and said,

"This is one of the great trees that Unos has said we must never take, and so Oné and I come here not. It is a powerful tree, above our order, and that is why I have not spoken of it to you."

"But Eva, I have eaten of this tree many times, it is wondrous. It grows plentifully in my kingdom and all the creatures of my land eat of its fruit and grow in wisdom. That is why I have come to you. I must explain so many things to you, because you and Oné are unaware and have never eaten of the fruit of this tree as I have."

"But Unos said we shall die if we eat of this tree."

"Am I not 'Life Giver' and do I not eat often of this tree? I am not dead. Indeed, I am a mighty king and a great heavenly prince Eva. I am of another world, because you have never seen of me before. I am from the world where Unos comes and we are the same. Does Unos not possess great wisdom and knowledge? He brings this knowledge to you from outside the Garden, where I dwell, and it is the knowledge that is stored in the fruit of this tree. Unos forbids you this tree, so that he can bring it to you and give you the knowledge.

"Has Unos indeed said you shall die or that simply you should not eat? For if you ate, would you not be like him, as I am, and be one with us? You shall become a god full of knowledge and wisdom and you will be a delight to Unos for he will embrace you as one like him."

Sa-Tan spoke many words and beguiled her with persuasive arguments until finally he stretched out his arm and gave Eva the glowing fruit. She held it in her hand and turned it over and around and it glowed on her face, in her eyes and on her cheeks.

"Eat of this tree Eva, and take some to your husband Oné, and I shall come to you, and we shall fellowship with Unos when he comes tomorrow on the seventh day. We will all eat together and grow in wisdom and be one. We surely shall not die. Has any creature in the Garden ever died?"

And with these words Shemgazi flew away from Eva. The woman stood looking at the fruit and turned over the words of Sa-Tan in her heart. She thought on him, how beautiful he was, how radiant, how gentle and wise his words seemed to her. And she accepted what Sa-Tan told her and ran to the massive tree and plucked several more of the fruits and ate of them lustily. They were indeed rich and luscious and she felt their warmth wash through her inner most being and burn warmly in her soul. Could anything that tasted so good bring death?

Eva ran back to the west where she knew Oné was and came to him. She held out some of the first fruits she had plucked. Oné said to his wife,

"what are these fruits Eva, I have not held them before, where do they come from?"

"They come from the center of the Garden, husband, the wondrous Red Shining One that I have told you about showed them to me. He gave me one."

Eva told Oné all the words that the Sa-Tan had spoken.

Oné sat while she spoke, and considered what she said.

"This is fruit from the Bloodred Tree that Unos has spoken of. He has forbidden us to take of this tree!"

Oné was troubled, yet considered the words Sa-Tan had given his wife, and they seemed good to him despite his unease. He desired wisdom so that he might please the LoGoi. Oné surmised he might give a gift to Unos in return for all the gifts he had received. He wished to surprise Unos, yet he knew not why the LoGoi had forbidden the taking of this tree.

Oné looked at the fruit in his palm for a long time, slowly turning it over and over, observing its glow. He considered Unos's words not to eat, but thought about the knowledge the strange creature had promised. He looked at Eva and saw that she had not died and how good she said the fruit was. Indeed it shone and was luscious and red.

After a long time, Oné finally decided.

He believed Eva and the Shining One as he looked at his beautiful wife, at the fruit, and doubted in his heart the LoGoi. Oné bit deep and hard into the lush red flesh and the red juice ran down his chin and stained his side and belly above his rib. It was warm. Strength flushed into his limbs, and his mind cleared and he could see, but it was not good. His loins began to burn and he looked down and noticed his manhood had become strong and changed. He looked over and saw Eva differently than before. He saw her weakness, and strange emotions welled up within him. It grew cold and dark and there were rumblings in the east and under the ground.

The Sa-Tan watched from afar, deeply concealed, and a broad smile stretched across his face as the juice sluiced down Oné's porcelain flesh and into his groin. The Sa-Tan threw back his head and laughed a deep and evil laugh full of victory, satisfaction and contempt.

Oné and Eva were startled by the sudden cooling of the things. The canopy above them darkened and the light faded. The animals became noisy and restless and began to agitate in the trees and forests around them. Something was wrong.

Oné stood up and dropped the fruit. It splattered on the ground, its bright flesh fading as the juice seeped into the earth. A thin ribbon of red ran down Onés' body. He felt cold and afraid, and looked at Eva and realised they were naked. He had always felt safe, but now he felt empty and exposed inside. He ran, and ran and ran through the forest, yelling and shouting and screaming while Eva ran after him. He was fearful and confused. His kingdom had changed and he could feel his power and confidence ebbing away. Oné felt somehow cut off and falling away from everything he had understood and known.

"We have done a terrible thing, wife! I am afraid!! We must hide ourselves, for Unos comes at the dawn."

Oné gathered the large fleshy leaves of a giff bush and wove the leaves into a cape that covered his erect person. He made one for Eva too, so that Unos would not notice his change, for it confused him.

They lay together all that sixth night, and the Garden cooled and darkened and strange noises came from the east. In the morning, as the dawn rose, Oné was gripped with panic. Afraid to face Unos he took Eva by the hand and they fled to the southern reaches of the Garden and sunk themselves in the warm marshes amidst dense flowering reeds.

The mighty LoGoi came and walked beneath the trees. He knew where Oné was, but he called to him nevertheless, waiting for the man and woman to respond to him. But they did not; instead they hid themselves. Unos walked up and down the banks of the marshes beneath the trees and called and called out across the waters but there was only the rustle of the reeds. All day Unos called. Night fell and Unos departed. It was the first seventh day in which there was no fellowship between God and man.

Well after dark, and when they were sure Unos had gone, the man and the woman drew themselves out of the warm waters. The giff leaf capes Oné had fashioned were sodden and their bodies were shrunken. Their skin was blotched and they were cold. They returned to their nest and saw that all the leaves had faded and this alarmed them. Fearsome noises came to them from the animals in the forests and pastures around them. They clasped each other and held one another tight. In their closeness Oné loved Eva with his body and entered her difference and that night in the cold and darkness as they tried to drive away their fear they conceived a man-child, the first human of the earth.

On the dawn, the eighth day, Unos came to them unexpectedly, for he had never come to Oné and Eva outside the seventh day.

"Oné where are you, I searched for you but did not find you."

Oné was ashamed but he came to Unos beneath the trees and cowered. Unos lifted him up and looked in to his eyes.

"Why are you shaking Oné, and where is your wife?"

"The woman you gave me, whom you bought to me in the Garden. She did give me to eat . . . and I am changed. I am now naked."

"Who told you that you were naked?"

"I am naked my Lord and Eva also, we are changed and we are cold. We see and understand things that give us fear."

"Have you eaten of the fruit of the Bloodred Tree, Oné?"

"I have eaten. The wife you gave me made me eat,"

and the man dropped his head and hid his eyes from the LoGoi.

"You brought her in to the Garden. I would not have eaten if but for Eva."

"Do not blame your wife Oné, for you ate of your own mind, while she was deceived. You chose for yourself. You doubted me and believed another whom you have not known. You did not trust me Oné, you questioned my love and my Word. You listened to your wife Eva who was deceived by a false one. Where is your wife?"

Oné went and found Eva and brought her before the LoGoi.

Unos looked sternly at them both and anger rose. He turned to Eva,

"You have done a terrible thing Eva. You have brought disobedience and untrustworthiness in to your line. You are with child. You will bring forth a man and his coming will be a great pain to you, because of what you have done. You will suffer the tumults of trusting the snake instead of trusting your loving God." And turning to Oné, he said, "you have chosen to be accursed Oné. We are separated you and I. I will depart from you and you and your wife will be driven from this Garden. You will be shrouded with toil, trouble and sweat because you chose to live by the fruit of the Bloodred Tree and not by my Word and in my love."

Taking their shrunken hands, Unos said to them,

"Why have you covered yourselves?"

"We are ashamed Lord," said Oné.

"For now the men that you say will proceed from us, will be cold as we have become cold, and will see and know the things of fear. For this reason we are ashamed of our glory parts and I did not want you to see our change.

"You gave us these parts as partners with you in creating things on the earth. And now because of what we have done, they shall be cold, and accursed, and we are ashamed, so we have covered them, our nakedness."

"You shall no longer be covered this way," Unos said,

"And though I drive you out, yet before I depart shall I cover you."

Unos took two innocent lambs from their home, for Eva loved lambs and Unos slew them. Their blood flowed out over their white wool even as the fruit of the tree had stained Oné's porcelain white skin. This appalled Oné and Eva, who had never seen such a thing. The lambs were the first creatures ever to die. They were innocent but Unos killed them both for the sake of Oné and Eva. The LoGoi took the skins and crafted them in to lovely soft garments, one for Oné and one for Eva. But he left the blood on the inside so that blood was against the skin of them both. When they were clothed they were stained with the blood of each lamb, blood red like the tree. The LoGoi did this, as a reminder to them of what they had done, in staining themselves with the red juice of the Tree of the Knowledge of Good and Evil. He clothed them in garments with the blood un-scraped from the inside but on the outside they were white as wool. This Great Thing of Heaven was concealed from all, except the Father and Unos the Faithful One who understood the plans of the Father for the future–a plan for redeeming by reddening.

The LoGoi Unos covered his children Oné and Eva in skins. And he wept. And they wept sorely and cried with great gushing sobs, and they sunk to the ground and held each other. But the LoGoi kissed them both and left them, though tears were in his eyes. He sped immediately by air to the great white tree of Eternal Life in the north, and he covered it with a dense fog and surrounded the land about the mighty tree with thickets and thorns. He made it so that no man could break through to the Tree and eat of its fruit thereby living perpetually as the angels do but locked forever in disobedience, shame, loss and cold with no faith and trust in God.

As night fell that eighth day, there was a fearsome war in the forests of the Garden as animal turned against animal and tore each other, and consumed each other, for they too were stained with the madness of the Bloodred Tree. Every time they ate of the tree's red fruit, they were consumed by rage, and hunger, and they attacked and tore at each other to satiate themselves. There were fearsome shrieks and roars and animal sounds all around so that Oné and Eva were frightened beyond measure, though God had given them charge over all the creatures, great and small. Now the two, man and woman, feared them. The animals no longer came to them, but were afraid, and they fled from Oné and the Garden, and from each other, and were spread all over the flat table of the earth according to their types. The great ceratopsians in their herds, the sauropods, the mighty flying creatures, and all the small and furry animals departed the Garden God had planted for the man and woman in the east. They were ever at war with one another and attacked and ate each other to satiate a gnawing hunger within. They existed in fear, and vanity and strife. Peace fled from the order of created things of the fourth and fifth days.

During the tumult of the night and the bellowing and crying of all the beasts and birds and creatures of the Garden, a frightening light came to where Oné and Eva lay concealed and shuddering in their despair.

Two mighty cherubim came to them with flaming swords, Raphael and Gabriel, the cherubim of Watching and Words. They advanced towards the man and the woman, and Oné and Eva fled from them in the night for the cherubim and their flaming swords were terrifying to them beyond imagination. Gabriel and Raphael followed Oné and Eva until they reached the borders of the great Garden where wild pastures spread out towards the west, and the man and woman fled in absolute panic down the trails and out onto the Great Plain. The two cherubim with flaming swords stopped at the lush edge and there they stood, guarding the way back into the Garden. While they were there, God the Father uprooted the great white tree of Eternal Life and it ascended up in to the canopy and disappeared. Great was the noise of the rendering of it from the soil and a great depression is there to this day beneath the waters hidden beneath the ground where Phirst was.

But Unos was not done in the Garden. After Oné and Eva had fled, he flew to where the Sa-Tan had concealed himself deep under the ground. Unos drew Shemgazi's sinuous form out of the ground.

The LoGoi grasped Sa-Tan by the head and his wrath blazed like a universe of fires. He cast the Fallen One down before him. All his light departed and he coiled and splayed in the dust before his Creator and was terribly afraid.

"Because you have done this evil thing, no longer will you be called Shemgazi. I remove all your light! You shall be the Sa-Tan, the Red Dragon. No longer will you shine. You will be wrapped in darkness. You, Fallen One, shall be bound to the earth, and crawl spiritually through its dust even as you soared through the heavens in your arrogance before you were found discordant with your brothers and the Prince.

"How the mighty have fallen! I place you beneath man, and you shall fall in the end, joining your wicked master Apollyon-Abysso while man is exalted and embraced by the heavens. You shall be at enmity with man and will strike from under him, up at his heel in humility. The fruit of Eva will crush your head underfoot. There shall come a man who shall undo you entirely. But for the time left you, though you seek to exalt yourself, you shall crawl beneath mankind in the dust of this earth. You will desire man and his earth, but it will be at war with you. And your great undoing will come of the woman whom you deceived and lead astray, whom you tempted to eat of the Bloodred Tree. She shall have justice against you through a tree and the fruit of her womb."

Unos crafted a creature from the dust of the earth, and he called it "snake." He marked it with poison and fangs and released it to crawl beneath the earth in cracks and crevices and in the branches of trees. It was a sign to man of the Sa-Tan who had called himself "Life Giver" but brought only death. The Sa-tan was now beneath man in the created orders, such was his fall for deceiving man and woman with fruit from the branches of the Bloodred Tree. Unos took Sa-Tan's spirit and diminished it, and sent it into the snake, Sa-Tan crawled away, an extinguished flame.

The fallen seraph coiled in pain, groaned, and hid in filth and despair. The snake slithered away. His light vanished so that he was no more, his form withered and faded away so he could no longer be seen. But the snake continued and grew its poison and its cunning and stealth towards the animals of the field. Sa-Tan was marked and set in the created order of things in the earth, below the man and beneath his feet. He went about as an empty spirit in the earth, symbolised in the second order by the crawling snake that bites, and crushes, and crawls beneath the feet of man. Such creatures also sometimes gathered themselves into the branches of trees to be above man and so fall upon him, such is the instinct of snakes bound to the symbolism of the Sa-Tan.

As Shemgazi was undone, so too were the other Watchers, for his light was within each of them; they were bound to him with their shared light. They too were extinguished. His judgement was their judgement, for they shared their lights as one great evil. Across the world, in the skies, under the earth, in the rivers and on the high places which they loved the most, they were all undone. They were turned out across the earth in their territories across the table of the land as disembodied spirits. Across the whole flat expanse of the earth, except the ocean around it, for they feared the waters, snakes emerged from the ground. They waited, ready for the coming of the beasts of the earth and the children of men. The Watchers diminished in fear and pain, and their lights vanished completely, and like Sa-Tan they could no longer be seen. Unos judged them and removed their form other than in snakes, scorpions, and crawling things on the earth which are a symbol of their enmity with man and their place in the third order.

Unos departed. The Garden decayed and died and returned to the ground. The cherubim with the flaming swords remained there until the Garden and the Bloodred Tree were dust—that is, until Oné died—and then Gabriel and Raphael returned to their Gates before the Throne.

6

The Cube

Don't let the prophecies, ancient or modern,
Trap you in a box of fear and futility.
Change the dance by becoming the light that you are,
The light that continues through and beyond the box
Into the adventure of forever.

—Ruth Ryden

Lord Carnarvon. *"Can you see anything?"*
Howard Carter. *"Yes, wonderful things."*

—The opening of Tutankhamon's tomb

"This is ridiculous! It can't be! 5600 BC + or—400 years? It's wrong. Wrong! Wrong!" Vitruvius exclaimed.

Pollen grains and fossilised seeds extracted from the soil of the hole underneath the Coffee Pots had been matched to Paleolithic (Old Stone Age) strains of wild einkorn wheat, emmer, almond, oak and pistachio tree. These were all *cultivated* grain types known from the excavations of ancient sites such as Catal Huyuk, Can Hasan, Ugarit and Zawi Chemi Shanidar. The fossilised rat molars came in slightly younger at 4200 BC + or—400, but still, the results dated the hole to between 7000 to 8000 years old. This made Vitruvius' shaft one of the oldest human constructions on record. The dating of the Coffee Pots did not fit within accepted timelines or any cultural chronologies. Instead they fitted alongside the earliest known human habitations, such as the oldest layer of ancient Jericho, dated to approximately 9000 BC, the time of the earliest known farmers. The dates were 2000 years *before* the known city-states of Sumer or the emergence of writing in Mesopotamia, and two and a half millennia before the development of cuneiform writing or Egyptian hieroglyphic script. The results had to be wrong.

In order to answer his own questions, Vitruvius led the team excavating the bottom of the urn shaft. It was now wide enough that a man could be lowered down and squat in the bottom. The floor was carefully excavated to the bedrock under where the Coffee Pots had lain buried beneath a few feet of soil at the bottom of the hole. And then an amazing discovery was made.

Carefully excavating the surface of the shaft floor, graduate assistant Christine Garrat of Otago University, uncovered a second glyph carved in the bedrock. It had been impossible to see at first, but after the loose sand had been brushed away, careful observation of the stone bedrock revealed a twin to the glyph carved on the tunnel wall above the shaft.

'The Hilltop Strangler'

The second glyph found on the Codex' stone lid
by Christine Garrat in the floor of the twelve-foot shaft
immediately below the 'Coffee Pots'

The glyph was perfectly preserved and was in much better condition than its tunnel counterpart. It depicted a figure with a long flowing beard, almost to his feet standing on a hillock holding a gazelle and a goat by the neck in each hand. He wore a full-length garment represented as a square. It was of much finer work. He was nicknamed the "hilltop strangler." Brushing away the last of the sand and dust with finer brushes, the graduate assistant discovered a thin ridge around the floor glyph. Within fifteen minutes she had traced it in a perfect square with the glyph centered in the middle. Vitruvius was summoned from further down the tunnel, where he was assisting the extraction of the shaft-fill by relay to Mini Mesh. A buzz went around the tunnel team. The square ridge appeared to be the edges of a stone lid.

Before anything else was done, Vitruvius had a digital camera passed down and the exposed ridge and glyph were thoroughly photographed and measured by Christine Garrat. All data was called up to a recording staff member at the mouth of the shaft above.

Once this was done, she swapped places and Vitruvius descended into the bottom of the shaft to carefully review the find. He slipped the blade of 'Dundee' into the fine crack framing the glyph. He was able to force the knife further under and slowly lift the stone lid. It was heavy, and once ajar he slid a flat pinch bar in on top of the knife blade to take the pressure. He pushed down with his one free hand and the lid prised up. Vitruvius then pushed a small wooden chock underneath and rested the lid back onto the chock. The knife and pinch bar were removed and the process repeated on an opposite side of the lid. A cord was then tied four ways under the lid and it was carefully raised to the surface to be entombed in cotton wool. Boxed and 'mummified' it was despatched out through the tunnel to the Mini Mesh. With the lid safely evacuated, Vitruvius' hungry eyes turned to the square hole beneath.

Inside the one foot square hole, was a desiccated box just over ten inches square. The lid had rotted away and he could make out the remains of the sides, which had withered and collapsed as air rushed in from above. There, in the middle of the remains was a perfectly square cube of metal glimmering under the lights of the shaft. Its radiance played across his face and into his eyes.

"I see metal,"

his excited squeak escaping back up to the surface. The team on their knees around the hole looked at each other, mouths gaping open.

Vitruvius was beyond elation. His hands shook and his breath came in rasping gulps as he dared not even to breathe over the amazing find at his fingertips. He could just make out ancient runes carved into the surface. He felt his mentors looking over his shoulder.

"Well Heinrich and Henry. We've found a wonder!"[1] he said out loud.

Gingerly digging his gloved fingers around the metal block through the now ashen box sidings, he carefully lifted it out of the hole like a firstborn child. It was surprisingly light. As it came out he noticed the cube was horizontally inscribed down its outer edges. The metallic cube, excavated from a wooden box from a small twelve inch hole beneath five Canopic urns in the bottom of a twelve foot shaft at the end of a forgotten snaking tunnel off a non descript side wadi, would now dominate the rest of Vitruvius' life.

Other artifacts were found in and around the hole: a metal blade, small rocks of various worked shapes, and the imprint of textile forms in clay that had hardened and fossilized. From the imprints, a specialised team was able to deduce that weaving had been in practice and that the pattern of the woven material revealed a sophisticated level of manufacture. There had perhaps been screens or wall hangings in the tunnel, perhaps sacks containing heavy items that had sat up against wet clay or people wearing pants made of woven threads had sat on soft clay that had later hardened.

Later, a secondary team found the sides of two megalithic rocks where Vitruvius had first noticed the chisel marks. They were recessed into the sides of the tunnel like massive protruding ribs. An original lintel spanning the two megaliths had collapsed and was buried upright over the right hand megalith presenting more or less three large standing stones. The three upright stones marked the termination of the natural cave complex of alluvial stone and soil and the beginning of the hand cut rock tunnel beyond.

Jerome Ladsen, a senior archaeologist who had joined Vitruvius' team eventually excavated the megaliths that were dug out and removed with much difficulty. A shaft was sunk from above to extricate the megaliths by crane. Ladsen and his team went on to reconstruct a cross section of the entire site. It appeared there had been an original mound some several hundred feet from the wadi, built on a rock outcrop. Their

---

1. Heinrich Schliemann and (Arthur) Henry Layard.

careful topographic archaeology established that a small village had once existed on top of the mound, confirmed by the presence of domesticated animal bones, postholes and rudimentary stone tools. They theorised that the megaliths had originally framed a tomb that had been cut as a tunnel back into the solid rock. At a later stage a twelve-foot shaft had been sunk into the rocky earth at the end of the tomb and the cube interred in a box with the stone lid. The urns had probably been placed above the sealed box much later, perhaps even generations later, and the hole had filled up with dust and dirt over the eons. The tunnel system was probably an ancient tomb structure beneath the mound upon which sat the agricultural Early Stone Age village. Over the millennia, the regular floods of the wadi system had deposited several feet of thick sediment building up against the side of the mound and joining it with the stream where it was annually sliced away by floodwaters. The riverbed had risen several feet but not as high as the overspilled floodplain around it which now butted up against the original mound.

The hillock, tunnels and shafts were eventually swept clean by fastidious archaeologists. The area was eventually closed and sealed, and attention moved to the five Coffee Pots and the strange metallic cube known ever afterward as the Affluveum Codex.

After eighteen months, the Mini Mesh headed by Christine Garrat and Jerome Ladsen was closed and teams departed for various other sites around the world. During this time the cube was sequestered in a fine chemical bath to slowly clean the object. Loose ends were tied up and localised surveys concluded disclosing no other anomalies worth investigating in the vicinity. Within another six months, two full years after he had first followed the animal tracks, Vitruvius handed over the directorship of the Mesh to his most able graduate Christine Garrat. Jerome Ladsen stayed as well. He'd found more than an exciting past at the site; he and Christine developed a future together, based on their shared interest in archaeology. They later married and became something of a darling couple within the archaeological fraternity somewhat dominated by rustic bachelors. Vitruvius was confident Christine would continue the excavation of the agricultural and black obsidian-trading village of Nemrut Dag and draw out new knowledge. Vitruvius retreated to his base at the archaeological museum of Istanbul University on Beyazit Square and began his analysis of the cube and the Coffee Pots.

Over the course of time the five urns were revealed to hold the desiccated remains of five separate individuals dated to the late sixth millennium. No DNA was extracted from the remains. The one Canopic urn without a bung, 'Genesis,' and the stopped urns 'Exodus,' 'Leviticus,' 'Numbers' and 'Deuteronomy' perplexed and intrigued science for several decades. The material from which they were made was a new kind of fossilised alloy, a blend of iron ore and other metals that formed a much denser and purer metal unknown to modernity. Its discovery turned "Neolithic" and "Bronze Age" classifications on their heads.

The medium was classified "rock metal" as its consistency was like stone, yet it had been liquefied as molten material at some point. The four head bungs were of clay but had been soaked in a resin that permeated the texture of the wood and solidified and petrified the heads making them as hard as stone. Along with the dry mummifying conditions at the bottom of the shaft, the resin appeared to have preserved the objects.

Using an ultra violet luminescence technique, ancient fingerprints were discovered on the urns and oil was detected on the surfaces. The prints were later isolated to two individuals with the intriguing find that they showed them to be larger than a modern hand. The fingerprints came from a perfectly identical modern human hand but with a breadth of at least ten inches, making them enormous. The anatomy of one of the individuals was calculated by biological and physiognomical experts to be well over ten feet in height.

The prints revealed hands that had endured hard work, pockmarked by incisions, cuts and blemishes. Whoever had placed the urns in the shaft had been a hard worker. It was speculated that the second set of prints, smaller and more delicate, were those of a woman. The prints were affectionately labelled 'Urnest A' and 'Urn-Ester B.'

The various findings ignited a furore between the Evolutionist and Creationist fraternities and created interest among biblical scholars related to the text of Genesis six. The controversy placed the Nemrut Dag site artifacts at the center of archaeological debate for the next three decades. Vitruvius Affluveum studiously avoided such vanities and instead remained focussed on the crux of his life's work: the mysterious metallic cube known as the Affluveum Codex. Holed up in Beyazit Square behind the safe parameters of the university and a protective academic Board, he declined all requests for interviews, debates and articles, which only added mystique to his now considerable archaeological reputation.

This endeared him to the Turkish authorities following the still unpleasant after taste of the historic Dorcan affair and James Mellaart's discovery of Catal Huyuk. It also made Vitruvius Affluveum an enigma to pop-archaeology and added to his austerity within academic circles. The media frenzy surrounding the finds and their controversial dating propelled the Coffee Pots and the Codex to a level surpassing the fame of the Dead Sea Scrolls and the Rosetta Stone. They were, put simply, the darlings of 21st century excavation.

After eighteen months following the closure of the Mini Mesh, and safe behind the sanctuary walls of his conservatory buried in the labyrinth of the university, Vitruvius set to work. Using a powerful electron microscope provided by an American sponsor, Vitruvius first discovered that the horizontal rectilinear lines running right around the cube were not in fact inscribed lines, but the edges of *layers* sandwiched between thick top and bottom blocks. The top and bottommost 'pages,' were each 3 1/2 inches thick.

This discovery added to the seeming unending sensations that emerged around the findings and cemented Vitrvius' place in the historicity of archaeology. He had taken his place beside Schliemann, Layard, Evans, Carter and Champollion.

7

Kainos and the Red Death

*"You'll find it easier to be bad than good if
You have red hair," said Anne reproachfully.
"People who haven't red hair don't know what trouble is."*

—Lucy Maud Montgomery,
Anne of Green Gables

*Will all great Neptune's ocean wash this blood
Clean from my hand?
No, this my hand will rather
The multitudinous seas incarnadine
Making the green one red.*

—Macbeth II.ii

Oné and Eva fled westward in an attempt to separate themselves from the things that had taken place. They wanted to get away from the terrible cherubim that had followed them out. They fled in terror and put many miles between themselves and the Garden. Oné sought a well-watered place where they could settle, where he could rebuild and try to wipe the change away. He felt that if he could just find somewhere new, everything would be well; that a change of location would restore everything to the way it had been. But all was despoiled. Oné was to find no rest no matter where he wandered for the rest of his days. The Bloodred Tree was within him.

The animals moved out to all parts of the world, for now they were driven away by each other, and by the fear of man and the terrifying light of the cherubim with flaming swords.

After travelling for several days, Oné and Eva found a cave well fed by water and there they stopped, slept and shivered. Hunger eventually drove them out and, finding the fruit trees withered and the fruits spoiled, Oné killed a small raptor. In desperation they plucked it, pulled it apart and ate it raw. It disgusted them both, but Unos had told them to kill and eat, since the animals were given to them as food until they could nurture life-giving plants from the soil again.

Eva's belly grew as she helped her husband scrape a living from the dust using horns and wooden tools and whatever they could gather. Harsh berries sustained them, the abundant fish they could catch in the nearby stream and any animals they could trap. It grieved them sorely to kill and consume the creatures. Eva gathered fish and shells from the river and aquatic plants. She mashed them into a paste to which she added water in a bowl made of toughened hide and boiled by dropping in a stone heated from the fire.

In time they moved upriver and settled in a large rock shelter in the curl of the great river that wandered westward out from Phirst, with a spectacular vista over the plain below. When the time was right, Eva brought forth a child. She was wracked with pain and Oné despaired for her life. Blood flowed from her, for her chid was brought forth in fear and the blood-red juice of the great tree. Oné was greatly afraid, but he remembered Unos' promise, that Eva would bring forth a man-child. The blood and anguish disturbed them both. When the child came, he came with afterbirth and had a long string between himself and his mother Eva, which Oné severed and tied in a knot. Eva and Oné had no such thing and they marvelled at it, the sign on his belly. They buried the sacred flesh that came out with the child under a tree and named the man Kainos which means "Fruit of the Tree of Woe" and also "Child of Blood."

Oné and Eva had many sons and daughters for the LoGoi was with them, and their offspring grew quickly and spread out from that place across the table of the earth in family groups and tribes. Over time Oné and his sons and daughters gathered certain breeds of creatures to them. They tamed sheep and goat types, and the horned auroch, and dogs, and birds of various types, and various hoofed creatures that were plentiful and good to eat. They nurtured the soil and Oné and Eva and their children grew crops for food in the lush ground that spread in every direction. Unos had taught Oné the nature of all things before the taking of the fruit, and this the man applied to life and taught his sons and his sons' sons. Oné became a great farmer and shepherd of many animals.

Oné crafted weapons for himself, and with these inventions he killed the fearsome animals that were about. With packs of dogs he ran down the dangerous predators and killed the feathered raptors and oviraptors of all sizes and other beasts for food and clothing. The animals all feared Oné because of what had happened in the Garden.

After Kainos was born, Eva also brought forth A-Bel. A-Bel was a peaceful man and he toiled among the herds of creatures of Oné, which was also the name of their home. But Kainos was vexatious and an anxious man as he toiled in the soil. It was bitterness to him and it fed an angry heart. Kainos and A-Bel were elder brothers among the other sons and daughters of Oné and Eva, for they were the first. They had not known the former things, the glory of the Garden, just the cold and fear of the west, and the animals and decaying plants of the world. But Oné and Eva told them of all the things that were before, mostly of Unos and how he walked with them, and the coming of the Shining One, the Red Snake, who had tricked them.

Oné and Eva spoke often to their children about Unos; there were many tears because he no longer came to the earth. They taught their children to make gifts to God as a token of their love and each year at the harvest of the crops and when animals brought forth their kind, for things no longer happened continuously as they had, but in seasons. After the eating of the Bloodred Tree, life came in cycles that determined the life of man. Oné sought to make offerings of the best of his labours, to atone for his guilt and in the hope God would return to Him. And God looked down, and was gracious. He sent fire from above as a sign. It would consume their gifts, but Unos did not return to them. Oné wept this loss until the day he died.

The grace of the fire from heaven brought joy to mankind. The sons of Oné were awed by it, for they had not known the love of God. When they captured it, the fire warmed them and they understood God in it. Oné took the sacred fire each year, and with it people kindled their own fires and kept them burning until the next annual offering. This fire was the light of men and was carried out across the earth from fire to fire. In his heart, Oné was deeply broken in spirit by the loss of fellowship with Unos yet he felt God was with him in part through the fire. He meditated constantly the former things as he worked the herds and the ground, and grieved their passing and their loss. But all man had, was the fire from heaven at Onés where they lived. Oné would often sit, rocking back and forth on his haunches, gazing into the fire and singing the ancient songs.

As the years passed, Kainos grew strong and vigorous but was sullen and bitter, so laboured was his toil. He grew weary and scarred. But A-Bel accepted his lot and laboured amongst the soft animals and thanked God for what he had. When both men were of years, they came to the annual offering with their younger brethren and with their parents Oné and Eva.

On stones piled toward heaven, they lay down portions of their own harvests, as was their father's custom. The children of men laid up their offerings and fire came from heaven and consumed their gifts as well. But fire did not come upon Kainos' gifts while A-Bel's animals were burned and consumed with heavenly fire. Kainos felt humiliated and afraid because God did not accept his gift. He laid it up with contempt for God and with all grumbling and complaints. He resented what God had allowed to come to pass.

There was great rejoicing and the sons gathered around their older brother A-Bel, but everyone was grieved and perplexed for Kainos. He withdrew and grew sullen. His bitterness eventually turned towards A-Bel.

Kainos took to farming well away from A-Bel and his animals on the outskirts of Onés, but A-Bel's animals would come and eat of Kainos' fields and crops. This made Kainos resentful. He grieved his loss of status among the children of Oné and Eva and his pre-eminence as first son. A-Bel grew in respect among the sons of men but Kainos was disliked and grew ever more sullen and withdrew with his sons and daughters and their tribes.

One day in late summer when the grasses were dry, A-Bel's animals happened in to a plentiful crop belonging to Kainos, for in those days men did not fence or restrict growing things. When Kainos saw what A-Bel's animals had eaten and trampled, he was extremely angry and came looking for A-Bel. The two brothers argued. Kainos' bitterness and grief and the respect he had lost amongst his brothers along with his humiliation before God welled up inside his angry heart.

"Why did God not send fire on my gifts yet he consumed your animals? And now your animals come and take what little I have nurtured by the sweat of my brow. And YOU, brother, you rob from me respect as the First Son among our brothers and the sons and daughters of our Father and Mother. I diminish and you increase and you show contempt for me!"

Kainos was very bitter when A-Bel rebuked him, saying his heart was black. A-Bel admonished him to sacrifice to God with a right heart and then the sacred fire from the sky would also consume his gifts.

Sa-Tan drew near. He whispered to Kainos many words, the same words that evil prince Apollyon had whispered to Sa-Tan and his brother seraphs of the East Light. He drew Kainos' attention to a strong green tree bough lying on the ground nearby which looked like a green snake. When Kainos heard A-Bel rebuking him, his anger overwhelmed him, fed by the lies of the Sa-Tan. Taking the heavy green bough in his strong hands he attacked A-Bel. Abel, surprised and shocked, fell back confused, crying out to Kainos. But Kainos reigned down blows upon his brother and smashed his skull and face until his body was a mass of broken flesh and blood mashed in to the ground. Kainos was a strong man and he beat the body of his lesser brother for almost an hour, as if to assuage his pain and the frustration and hatred towards God into the very soil that brought him so much travail.

Kainos frothed at his exertion like a panting beast until he was covered in blood, A-Bel's pulp, dirt, sweat and filth. He looked like a beast rather than a man. He had no compassion for A-Bel or A-Bel's children or his father and mother, but thought only of his anger and his contempt for all things.

A-Bel was the first man to die. It pleased Sa-Tan well and he withdrew to his place and all the Watchers rejoiced. A-Bel's blood seeped in to the earth and his cries came up to God and teraphim brought his cries to the Throne. Then a very rare thing happened.

Unos came.

He came to Kainos and appeared to him.

The bloodied man was awestruck, for he had never seen Unos, but knew of him from the stories Oné and Eva had told them all. Unos shone brighter than the sun. he was golden, gleaming like molten bronze, and his thighs and feet were like shimmering silver wrapped in lightning. He had mighty wings of light that moved around and over him. His head was handsome and hair cascaded down over his shoulders. As he came to Kainos, he dulled his light; his terrible visage distilled and became as a man but one who was completely white like sunlight.

Still clutching the bloodied tree bough Kainos fell to the ground to shield himself from Unos' radiance.

"Kainos! Where is thy brother A-Bel?"

Kainos first words ever to his Lord were disrespectful and full of contempt.

"I do not know Great One, am I my brother's keeper?"

"Your brother lays yonder in the dirt drowned in blood, broken and vanquished by your anger and bitterness. If you had offered me gifts in thanksgiving and from the purity of your heart as your brother did, I would have accepted your gifts.

"But now your gift to me is the blood of A-Bel in the earth which you toil. His screams at being destroyed by his own brother have come up to me.

"What is that tree bough in your hand Kainos? Is it not a bough stained with blood even as the juice of the great Bloodred Tree stained your father's lips and side?

"You are wicked Kainos. I BANISH you from Onés and the presence of my fire. You will be driven from this place into the lonely wilds. Wherever you go, you shall not be able to settle because of A-Bel. I will curse the soil you toil, so that it brings you only a single crop. You shall ever be compelled to move. Men will curse you and chase you away because of the terrible thing that you have done. You will be far from them and will dwell in the wild lands amongst the wild creatures. They shall trample and eat your crops, and you will ever be at enmity with them."

Kainos was overcome with grief. He cried out to the LoGoi, and begged Unos,

"Please O My God, do not do this thing, for men will kill me even as I have killed A-Bel. Let me not become as A-Bel!"

Even in his grief Kainos was thoughtful only of his needs and welfare, and cared nothing for his dead brother A-Bel.

Despite bringing murder to the earth, Unos still loved Kainos and had compassion for him. "You *will* be driven from this place and *shall* be cursed by the soil. But I will mark you, so that no man shall take your life or destroy you as you destroyed A-Bel. Your hair shall be red, the fruit of A-Bel's veins which has poured out in to the soil and on your flesh. You shall be marked from your crown by the red of slain A-Bel. His lifeblood will be a symbol of the great tree from which your heart is fed. This will be a reproach to men. Whenever they see your red hair, they shall see A-Bel's blood and the fearsome fruit of the forbidden tree that their forefather ate. And they will flee from you.

"You shall carry this blood upon your head until the day you die and go to the soil as your brother A-Bel has done. But no son of man shall slay you because of the blood red with which you are crowned!"

Then Unos the mighty LoGoi drove Kainos and his people from his presence with a fierce windstorm and they went stumbling away towards the north, the dominion of DRKaVac. The wind confused the people of Phirst, and they did not see Kainos and his people depart from them in the storm. Eventually Kainos came to the land now called Nod of the black sands. The sands spoke to Kainos of his bitterness and the blackness of his soul and so he stayed in this place.

Kainos took the daughters of his sons and his son's sons such as he found there, and he had children by them, and they too bore the mark of Kainos by the generations, so that they were despised amongst men, and were driven away. The "Blood Men," as they came to be called, became a great people and spread towards the north and the west and went up into the mountains away from men who shepherd animals and herds. There the Blood Men, the red heads, cultivated bitter crops in the cool and rocky soils of the mountains.

The sons of Kainos made houses of wattle and woven saplings and covered them with the foliage of red trees, and bloodied skins. They painted their own skin with paints made of red juices and ochres and matted their red hair with ochre clays and became fearsome to behold. They hated animals and trapped and killed them and ate them raw and dwelt in caves amongst the mountains. They were a robust and strong people, but brutal and cruel. They killed animals where ever they went in hatred of A-Bel and tore the flesh and ate it without fire for they did not practise the annual offerings custom as did the other sons and daughters of Oné and Eva. They baked breads and cakes from what coarse grains they could raise from a reluctant soil, and were ever moving, for the soil did not give them food for more than a harvest because God diminished the soils wherever the people of Kainos went.

Over time the red people of Kainos grew vigorous from the meats they consumed and a great brow grew up over their eyes to shield them from the snows where they lived. They were athletic and became hunters and wandered everywhere killing and consuming and never settling. They departed from their brothers the children of Oné who ate fruits, and milked animals and cooked the flesh of their herded beasts and dwelt in buildings of stone and wood and mud, where there was music and stories.

The Kainoi, the Blood Men, became like beasts, savage, bitter and fearful. They resembled red monsters and men no longer went near the mountains in the north. Tales and legends were told to the children of the fearsome Blood Men of the mountains and they became a reproach.

A-Bel was never found. Oné, Eva and all his kin wept and it was a great mystery to them. Every time a sudden wind came up and drove towards the north they remembered his loss, for in such a wind he disappeared and Kainos and his kin suddenly moved away. And so life changed in Oné.

Men began to prosper and spread out across the lands, for women brought forth men frequently. From earliest times they had relations with their brothers and fathers and this was not an evil thing in those days. As they spread, they moved by tribes and clans into the lands over which Sa-Tan had appointed the remnant of the Watchers. The Watchers sat and waited for them, like snakes coiled beneath rocks on the ground and in cracks of the earth ready to strike them down.

8

The Affluveum Codex

But words are things, and a small drop of ink,
Falling like dew, upon a thought, produces
That which makes thousands, perhaps millions, think.

—George Gordon Byron

Words, like nature, half reveal and
Half conceal the soul within.

—Alfred, Lord Tennyson

The Affluveum Codex was not a solid block at all; instead it was a series of layered golden sheets as thin as paper that had fused together beneath the weight of the top and bottom blocks that formed protective outer covers. The world realised that a discovery of the utmost importance was before them. The unearthing of the Codex was viewed with the same level of wonder as the finding of the Rosetta Stone, the Dead Sea Scrolls or the mysteries emerging from the translation of the Te Amarna Letters, or the Gilgamesh and Atrakhasis Epics. The lessons of the management of the Dead Sea Scrolls had been learned six decades on, and Vitrvius moved quickly and democratically to establish an international team to bring the Codex's secrets to the world as quickly as humanly possible.

A team of international experts including ancient linguists, paleo-metalographers, culturalists, chemists, cryptologists, paleo-botanists, photographers, illustrators, and other technical specialists were gathered. Vitrivius appointed Professor Llewelyn Loess of Pennsylvania University to head a communications team to disseminate all information and field media interest so he could remained sequestered away dedicated to the decryption of the Codex. Loess was given the task of convening a series of symposiums tightly focussed on isolated aspects of the finds as information emerged.

The symposiums sequestered commentary and interest in the Codex away from the researchers and gave a wider circle of academia a sense of ownership of the Codex and the other artefacts associated with it. Once it was discovered that the Codex was actually a series of golden sheets layered vertically, world experts in chemistry and conservation were consulted to devise a plan on how to pry the layers apart and discover what was hidden within. Over the course of six months, ideas were canvassed and a proposal decided. In the meantime, Vitruvius gave his mind and colleagues over to analysis of the top block that formed the cover of the Codex.

On the ten inch square metal page were two columns of unknown text incised into the gold alloy medium. The lettering was very fine, angled and wedged but with a degree of curvilinear form.

The linguists and language teams–known affectionately as "Bletchley Park II" or 'BP2' for short, after the Allies' World War II code breaking teams–worked out a series of patterns indicating the writing ran from right to left. A German team with expert knowledge of southern Sumerian cuneiform theorized the text was a proto-type of north Akkadian. That meant it was related to Babylonian, Assyrian, Hebrew and ancient Arabic. They also identified some tentative resemblance to later Linear A pictographs known, but as yet un-deciphered, from ancient Mycenaean Greece and the earlier Minoan civilisation on Crete.

Armed with these guideposts, and pouring over detailed facsimiles of the top sheet, more patterns began to emerge. These were passed back to Vitruvius who oversaw the excruciatingly slow jigsaw puzzle they were trying to decipher.

In order to process and separate the thin golden leaves, the Codex was eventually lowered into a second bath of diluted natural acid soup carefully calibrated by the chemists. They deduced, correctly, that the chemicals would react with the gold while working against the molecular makeup of the impurities holding the layers together. Over time, submerged in the chemicals, the 'glue' would dissipate and the alloy leaves would be free to be pried apart.

Over the course of two years, the synthetic chemical soup seeped in and dissolved the interleaved patina and released 365 leaves from each other. Eventually the layers were able to be painstakingly parted and placed in separate preserving baths before being naturally dried and vacuum sealed between sterilised glass plates. Like the topmost layer, the individual leaves also contained writing, running in two vertical columns.

Vitruvius had each leaf color photographed and the complete 365 facsimiles blown up twice their actual size, and pasted in a continuous frieze around the walls of the main conservatory. Above and below it, were pasted black and white facsimiles, in the same scaled size, of the Gilgamesh and Atrakhasis Epics as well as the Tell Amarna Letters for anyone to peruse and muse over. He had the communications team publish the facsimiles on an early form of the internet.

The glass plates with their precious cargo safely sandwiched inbetween, were laid on bleached white cotton tablecloths, end to end in two long columns. Each faced north and south on each side of a specially constructed table dominating the large conservatory. There they remained as an entombed vacuum-sealed treasure. To unravel the runes, Vitruvius contrived a series of teams. To a duo of two experts he gave a single facsimile of one page to decipher. Known as 'Singles' their job was to identify and single out any patterns, repeating clusters of letters, or anything unusual on their individual page.

Within BP2, Vitruvius established a second tier of teams each comprising five experts. 'Tight Fives' (named after the five players of a rugby front row charged with pushing forward) were given five sequential facsimile sheets per team to deduce patterns and identify development across the sheets.

'Trinity,' a third tier consisted of Vitruvius himself, Professor Zhou Tang of Peking University who had linked the tunnel glyph to ancient Chinese symbols, and Professor Gloria Ormond of the British Museum in London. Each moved up and down the master plates as well as floating among the Tight Fives and Singles monitoring finds and matching ideas in a coordinating whole.

Vitrivius rotated the scholars through BP2 so that everyone had an awareness of what their neighbors were doing and all had an overview of the whole. In this way a number of breakthroughs were achieved through shared observations and the matching of work being done by each separate group.

The color facsimiles were loaded into a high-powered computer database and screened at life size, catalogued and each given a number from *ACode* 1 to 365. In an anteroom off the main work area was a den of computers and analysts who collated the observations and patterns uncovered by BP2 Singles, the Tight Five cryptologists and Trinity. During night shifts, computer geek undergraduates were given access to the computerised facsimiles and invited to scroll through the database jotting down notes of anything they observed or found intriguing. In this way, a number of other keys came to light that helped unlock the Codex's cuneiform-style writing.

Loess and the Communications Team also managed a database of findings suggested by outside experts reviewing the facsimiles online from across the globe. These were cross referenced and discussed at BP2 round table meetings held every Monday morning in a conference room off the main conservatory.

The Codex contained thousands of ancient words, inscribed on 365 sheets of paper-thin gold alloy leaves. The chemists announced that the Codex was not in fact pure gold, but was made of an unknown yellow 'platinum' alloy close to electrum (gold and silver). This unknown alloy was eventually classified "Nemrutium" (Nu) after the name of Nemrut Dag where it had been discovered.

Everyone struggled to comprehend the metal technology that had created the Codex, buried in soil for perhaps 8000 years. But here before them were the irrefutable results, checked and rechecked by competing scholars. The results forced scholars and publishers to update histories and timelines everywhere. The findings punched massive holes through the crumbling nineteenth and early twentieth-century contrivances of "Neolithic," "Bronze" and "Iron Age" partitions. It was clear that here, in ancient Turkey, just outside the Fertile Crescent, had lived a people of sophistication advanced by several thousand years. The results angered many scholars, who attacked the findings. But over three decades, the scrutiny and peer review confirmed the original facts.

Scientists had known of gold foil from ancient Egypt, a soft metal easily hammered leaf thin. But paper-thin metallised sheets that could hold writing, demonstrated a level of technology that shattered all the conventions about human development. Scholars were left scratching their heads. The earliest known smelting of naturally occurring copper (Cu) was known in Anatolia (ancient Turkey) around 6200 BC and in the Balkans by 4500 BC and arsenical bronze (a simple two-third to one-third alloy of copper mixed with tin) from 3800 BC. The sophistication of the mysterious gold alloy was at least two to three millennia premature.

Electron microscopic analysis demonstrated that each sheet had been layered five times vertically and horizontally and hammered or pressed together to paper thinness. This technique resembled the way papyrus was made of opened reeds layered and beaten together or ancient samurai swords tempered in fire, layered and beaten over and over again until the metal reached the strength of steel. The technique had given each leaf a textured strength that held its shape despite its thinness.

Vitruvius was less concerned with the makeup of the material, however. Instead, his mind burned over the words and the *meaning* of the text. He wanted to know, above all else, what was written on the pages. His considerable skills became honed and coalesced around this driving motivation. He prioritised and delegated major responsibilities to avoid any distractions. Single-eyed management, along with his utter dedication, was what allowed the unlocking of the Affluveum Codex over the next twenty-seven years. Without his discipline and persevering obsession, the hidden text may never have come to light.

Like the Greek Linear A writing, the language of the Affluveum Codex was not immediately identifiable. Over time the excruciating work of BP2 honed it down to language groups within the Caucasus and Zagros mountains as well as early proto-Akkadian language groups of the Mesopotamian plain. The ancient languages of these locations shared certain structural aspects and compositional repetitions with Codex writing. Certain outcomes, when tested against several hypotheses also strengthened connections with the ancient Linear A pictographs of the ancient Aegean to the southwest.

Vitruvius allowed the best linguistic minds from across the globe to join the senior BP2 teams on a regular basis. They oversaw various teams charged with different departments of the code breaking strategy. They were all sworn to secrecy and signed a binding non-publication or reportage covenant in order to be able to work on the effort. Unlike the photographs, Vitruvius did not wish to leak out tentative interpretations of the text or dribble the decipherment in a piecemeal fashion. He endured speculation in the media, but there was no formal or even unofficial comment from his academic centre in Istanbul.

It took thirty-two years.

9

The Nephaliim come forth

Midnite: [to John] *I thought I heard thunder last night.*
Must have been Satan's stomach growling.
Gabriel: *Lucifer!*
Satan: *This world is mine—in time.*

—Constantine (2005)

And it came to pass, when men began to
Multiply on the face of the ground, and
Daughters were born unto them, that the
Sons of God saw the daughters of men
That they were fair;
And they took them wives of all that they chose.

—Genesis 6:1, 2

... she spawned monster-serpents,
Sharp of tooth, and merciless of fang; ...
Fierce monster-vipers she clothed with terror,
With splendor she decked them, she made them of lofty stature.
Whoever beheld them, terror overcame him,
Their bodies reared up and none could withstand their attack.
... hurricanes, and raging hounds, and scorpion-men,
And mighty tempests, and fish-men, and rams;
They bore cruel weapons, without fear of the fight ...
After this fashion, huge of stature, she made eleven [kinds of]
  monsters ...

—The Babylonian Enuma Elish

*Fee, fi, fo fum,
I smell the blood of an English man,
Be alive, or be he dead,
I'll grind his bones to make my bread.*

—Old English fairytale,
Jack and the Beanstalk

After the destruction of A-Bel and the casting away of the Kainoi, the Sa-Tan gathered the Twelve. They came to Mt Hermon, for the whole earth was one land, and Hermon was its center. It was here that Sa-Tan had established his seat. He ruled below the ground, above the ground, and in the air. Sa-Tan moved his throne about the earth. This was the first place it was established after the Twelve crawled from their fiery hole of undoing in the crust of the earth. Sa-Tan had conceived a great evil against Unos and creation. The fallen seraph told his servants what Unos had said to him, speaking of the woman who would bring forth a powerful man that would crush the head of snakes.

The Watchers talked long on Hermon of women and the man to come. Having been cast from the heavens, they envied the world, and looked upon the daughters of men, even as Sa-Tan had considered Eva by the azalea pools. The Watchers agreed they would take the daughters of men and make children of their own, to take and possess the earth and destroy the men. They would destroy the second order of creatures and would make their own race to live on the earth and rule over them as gods. By this evil they planned to overthrow women and prevent the coming of Snake Crusher.

The twelve fallen Watchers drew together and, biting into each other's souls, blended the remnants of light that remained within each one. The Watcher light coalesced and solidified as mass beneath the throne of Sa-Tan. There was sufficient light for six of the twelve Watchers to make form, like that of men, yet more glorious, larger and more terrifying. These six spread out across the earth from that place. Revelling in their newly accomplished physicality, they sought out women and corrupted them with violence. The six, like their brothers and the Sa-Tan, were cruel and hateful. Above all, they were proud. The disembodied Watchers that remained observed their six physical kin and drew life from their terrible acts. Within each of the six that had form was the immortal light of their disembodied brothers. Whether in form, or in spirit, the Watchers were joined together in ungodly acts upon the earth, joined by the remnant of their immortal light.

The corrupted daughters of Oné gave birth to children from the seed of the Watchers. Their offspring, only males by birth and sterile, were exceeding strong and grew to great stature. These became the ancient men of renown, the heroes of old lauded in the tales and legends of ancient peoples. These creatures were half men, half gods. They were cursed with an inner hunger unknown to men, that raged within them like fire. This hunger became a great curse to men, one which Sa-Tan conceived upon the earth.

> The Cannibals that each other eat,
> The Anthropophagi, and men whose heads
> Do grow beneath their shoulders.[1]

The Watcher known as JNN returned to his dominion in the far east and there found fair women of the family of Zamzummin. He came to some daughters by a lake in the evening. The women were afraid of his radiance and his strength. JNN took advantage of their fear and took them all violently like a giant fish sweeping through schools of lesser fish in the ocean. He trampled them down like a rampant ox in fields of wheat, laying it all down. The Watcher carried them all off. He ravaged and raped, so exuberant was he in his new physical form. He was most savage until they were all with child. He enslaved these poor creatures in a high place, where men had not yet come so that they served him completely. JNN ruled over them like a ravaging beast.

> There is no birth
> Of all things mortal
> Nor end in ruinous death;
> But mingling only and interchange of mixed
> There is,
> And birth is but its name with men.[2]

> Greet insolence with outrage.[3]

---

1. William Shakespeare, *Othello*.
2. Empedocles, Fragment.
3. Archilochos, Fragment 71.

66 THE BLOODRED TREE

The Nephaliim come forth

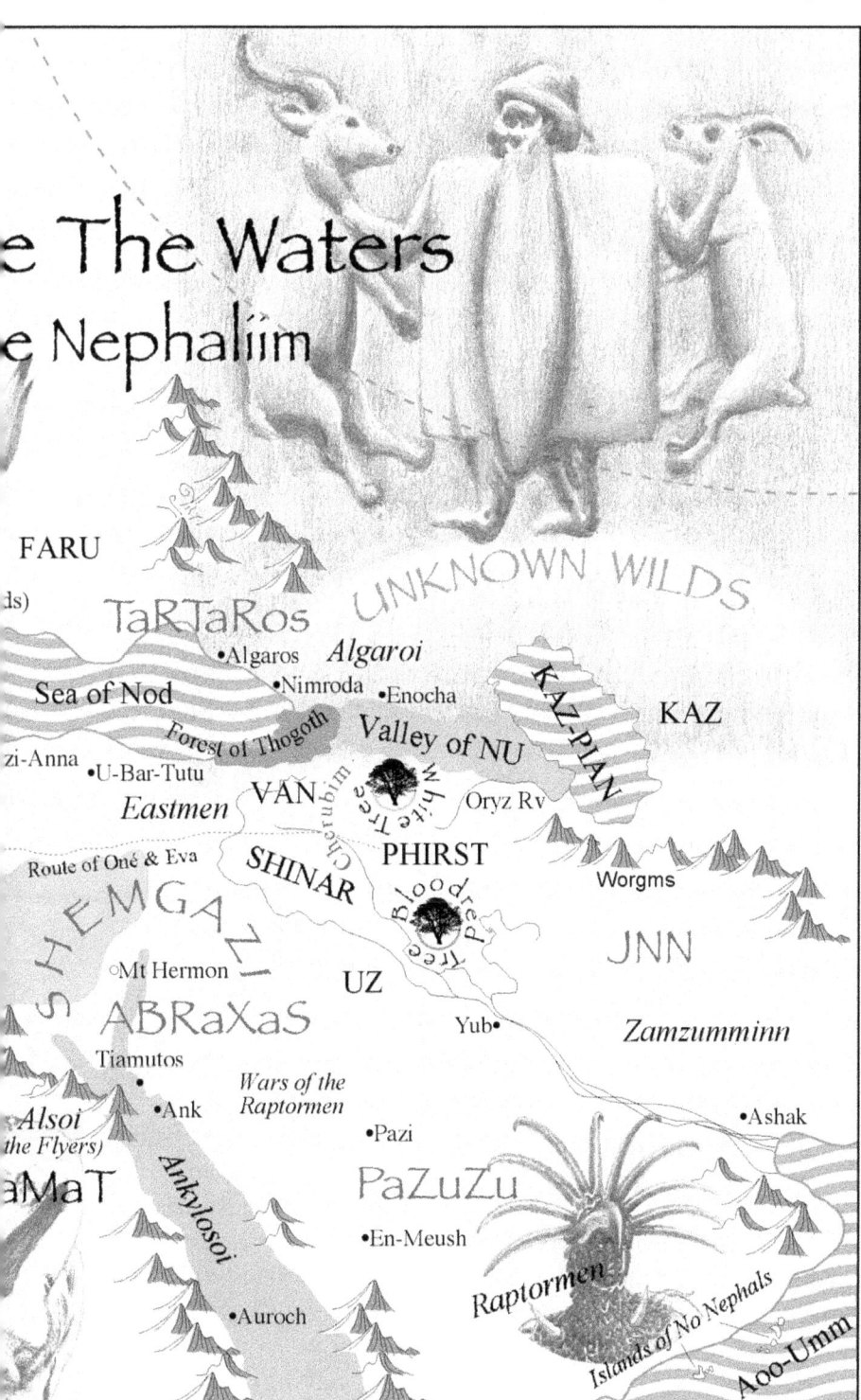

From time to time as it pleased him, he descended from his high plateau and killed such men as he found and devoured them. The women he treated differently, for they were fair to his eye. The daughters of Oné were very beautiful in those days. JNN spared them and took them away to his high place, for they gave him sons. JNN and his brothers lusted after women and continually ravaged them. Children were born to JNN and the other five Watchers who had form, the Watchers of Flesh. The offspring of these unholy unions were misshapen and ugly, yet powerful and very tall.

The sons of JNN, PaZuZu, DRKaVaC and CHaRuN, ABRaXaS, INCuBu–the six Watchers who took earth form–came to be called the "nephals," or "nephaliim," that is, the "giant fallen ones." These half men half gods–for they were neither angels nor men–spread out from that place and overpowered human beings and enslaved them. The nephaliim forced the children of Oné to grow crops for them and to fish and to husband and hunt animals and by whatever means bring them food. Men laboured up from the plains to the high paces, for the nephaliim set up their dominions on high places on the earth, reaching to the heavens where their fathers had once dwelt. Men laboured with burdens on their backs, hauling wagons and loading great beasts that they drove up to the nephaliim. The children of Oné ate only the scraps they could find after all was consumed by the hungry nephals.

Throughout the dominions of the Watchers, their sons the nephaliim grew gradually in number and spread out and gathered to themselves whatever groups of men they could find and enslaved them. The nephaliim considered themselves as gods, for men feared them. The nephaliim idled away in luxury built on the forced labour of men. The ungodly spawn lolled about on great pillows and textiles woven by women, and lived in huge stone buildings on high places. These beasts continually consumed the foods that men brought to them. They grew massive and fat and were completely evil.

In idleness the nephaliim contrived wicked sports and evil pastimes that caused great despair to men. Living men were killed or maimed and hung around their corrals on hooks and branches. When their bodies decayed they would be replaced with freshly impaled bodies so that the corrals were continually supplied with fresh victims that satisfied the cruelty and sadism of the nephaliim who hated men. There was complete injustice and no relief from the nephaliim. Men were enslaved and oppressed and laboured continually to feed the terrible giants.

But more children were born to men. The nephaliim were sterile and the Watchers of Flesh could not bring forth women, for Eva came out of Oné and was flesh of his flesh, bone of his bone, and the glory of man. So, they ate them and the parents of men who brought forth children. They also destroyed them in cruel rituals and tormenting sports of fire. In some places where the tribes of Kainos had farmed, the ground could no longer sustain crops and the wild animals departed. Food ran out and the nephaliim attacked and ate all the people. They also set forth and captured and enslaved new peoples. By this travail, the departure of animals and the lack of food caused the nephaliim to spread out across the table of the land.

This was a time of great oppression throughout the earth. Sa-Tan dispossessed humanity of its sovereignty of the earth and became the Prince of the Age. Those of the fallen order of Watchers from the East Gate of the music of Apollyon worked their malice against men, and propagated their vile counter species on the earth. By this means all men fled to the outer recesses of the Great Plain. They came eventually to the dominions of ZeMu, AZaZeL, TiaMaT, JNN, DRKaVaC and PaZuZu. But even there they found no relief, for wherever they came, above them, below them and amongst them was ever a Watcher. The nephaliim followed men as they migrated. The Watchers of Flesh took such daughters of man as they wished and made new nephals as people came into their dominions, so that men were never free. Sa-Tan and his Fallen Ones ruled from their strongholds throughout the table of the earth in a spiral around the seat at the center.

The sons of the Watchers, who could make no daughters of their own, were evil, arrogant and proud, wicked beyond measure. Great wars flourished among men and the nephals. These beasts of Sa-Tan cultivated vast armies of people and hurled them at each other. Armed people with terrible weapons were fostered and cultivated from nephaliim technologies and spiritual knowledge that they received from their fathers, the Fallen Ones. The mothers of men bred and were consumed like enslaved breeding mares, until they were overwhelmed and broken from the baring of so many monstrous and evil hybrid sons. The tears and deep groaning of women on the face of the world came up to God who was grieved by all the pain he saw on the face of the earth.

Wars raged across the land between the tribes of nephaliim who fought each other for the resources of the earth. They were fed by an unquenchable hunger and thirst, which was a spiritual fire within them. They had no soul, no sense of belonging in any created order, and this was an unquenchable thirst they could not quench. There were also wars among the peoples of the earth who fought over what was not consumed by the nephals.

There was a nephal called Og-Baal of PaZuZu. In one day he would eat: three wagonloads of baked breads; two wagon loads of slaughtered animal carcasses; and ten people or children (for he loved their struggling and screams as he tasted them and fed off their torment); a wagon load of dead birds of the air; and ten baskets of eggs of birds of the air. Og-Baal would eat three boats of fish or creatures of the swamps and marshes, including the ten-foot-long diadectes, which were eaten raw and seized upon, so tasteful was the flesh of these aquatic creatures. All these foods were gathered to his high place. It was a temple made of mud and stone and the bones of eaten men and vanquished beasts. The food would be brought up daily to the gateway of the high house, up a winding step trail of mud, dirt and blood and dumped at his gateway. He would fall upon it and consume everything, even sometimes the men who brought it up.

Men everywhere became numb under the oppression. Their hearts cried out to God, but they did not reach out to him, for they were lost and overwhelmed.

After many years, people grew scarce where the nephallim raged because of the wars and because the nephaliim consumed everything. The six Watchers of Flesh fell upon the great beasts and perverted and distorted even the orders of the animals with their seed, so that many of the creatures of the land became infected with the corrupting seed of the Fallen Ones as well as men.

The Watchers also took animals to themselves as wives and this caused the blood of animals to become corrupted over generations, with terrible things occurring in their created orders. They became loathsome, while others became sterile and departed from the earth. The bones of beasts failed them. They laboured in the earth under various distortions and weaknesses. Some creatures sprouted great horns as their skeletons exploded with despair and distortion from their evil blood: the styracosaur, the me-galoceras, mammut, mastodon and the ceratopsians. Others developed massive teeth such as the allosaurs, albertosaurs and the tyrannosaurs as well as the great cats, smilodon and the sabre-tooths with which to rend and torment each other. Others developed massive bony plates under which they were burdened: anklo-saur, with his mighty clubbed tail, and stegosaur, and colosso-chelys hiding beneath his great bony bowl. The great flying beasts would attack men and beast as the hunger and fire from the seed of the Fallen Ones raged through their bodies. But the Fallen Ones did not pervert the orders of the sea, for the sea was like the great Abyss and this they feared; they did not go in to that place nor pervert the creatures of the deepest waters.

Huge fires raged across the earth and the lands were blackened. Pits grew deep into the ground. Evil gas and molten fire came up from within and spewed out across the land. Smoke and fire, fed by all the trees cut down by the nephaliim as they taught men to make metals, blocked the sunlight God had given the earth. Men built ingenious constructions with which to serve the nephaliim gods and to torment man and beast. Terrible machines went out across the lands and brought great suffering to all living things.

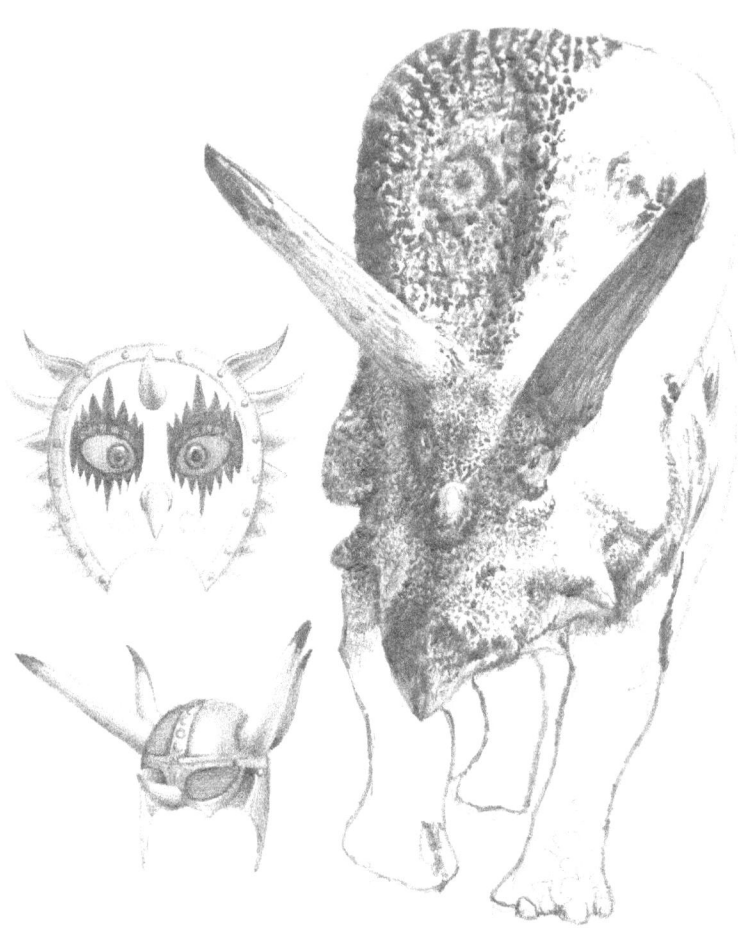

The Algaroi (Ceratopsia)

Cultural accoutrement of the Algaroi (Ceratopsia) Hu-Man tribes
and a bull ceratopsian

The Nephaliim come forth 73

A spiked Styracs

Warrior of the Styracs people from the fourth and fifth generations,
the time of the empires of Ammel-Uanna (in the South) and Ammel-Galanna (in the West).

Raptorman

A warrior of the sixth generation, the time of Du-Muzi.

The Nephaliim come forth   75

Alsoi and Ankylosoi
Warriors of the Alsoi (top) and Ankylosoi Hu-Man tribes

10

Evil Men and the Breaking of the Earth

Two sons were born to Eber:
One was named Peleg (which means "division")
Because in his time, the earth was divided.

—Genesis 10:25

Your servants are half dead, you're down to the bone
Tell me, tall men, where would you like to be overthrown . . . ?
I see pieces of men marching; trying to take heaven by force
I can see the unknown rider, I can see the pale white horse.

—Bob Dylan, *Angelina*

When the nephaliim were not killing and destroying men, they netted and trapped the great creatures God had made. The first to vanish from the face of the earth were the great sauropods. Although this grieved God greatly, the Fallen Ones rejoiced, for they enjoyed God's pain. Their malice for him burned deeply. The Watchers devised all manner of means to destroy all that was good that God had made in the beginning. They yearned to possess the earth especially having lost their natural habitation in the heavens and because of the great discord of which they were guilty.

In all the days of men before the Waters came in the times of the nephaliim, there were ten generations of men. The nephaliim took the most evil and mighty men as sons, because they could not create offspring of their own, and made allies of them. Together they conspired to do wicked things on the earth to their brothers, and to the animals and fish and birds of the air. Each generation brought forth its own evil men and they were raised up by the nephaliim as sons to rule and reign as chief men of the earth in that generation. But they were destroyed in the wars of the nephals. The nephaliim used them as pawns to assist with their evil deeds. After the second generation of men, that is, from the time of En-Ocha there were eight chief men on the earth who reigned as kings. Their names by their generations were, after Oné and Kainos, in the generation of En-Ocha,

> Al-Algar who is also called Nim-Roda
> Ammel-Uanna
> Ammel-Galanna
> Du-Muzi
> En-Meush-Um-Galanna
> Ensi-Pazi-Anna
> Enme-Du-Ranki
> U-Bar-Tutu, also called Zi-U-Sudra, who perished
>   with his armies when the Waters came.

Each of these fought with other men of the earth and warred against lessor kings. These men defeated them all and became the chief Hu-Man before Sa-Tan. They were each considered the mightiest war man on the earth in their generation and were blackened and merciless of heart, driven by arrogance and a lust for power over others.

In the north within the generation of En-Ocha—that is, the third generation—arose Nim-Roda. He was the first chief man to gather vast numbers of men to himself and to ally himself to the strength of the nephaliim who adopted him as a son.

Nim-Roda's captains devised orders amongst men and organised themselves into fighting armies styled after the great herds of animals that inhabited the earth. The Algaroi wore triple-horned helmets and held large two-eyed shields and called themselves the Ceratopsia. They flashed and shook their great shields that resembled the great frills of the ceratopsians. The Ceratopsia devised dances and customs that mimicked the walk and play of these great animals.

Men built great machines of wood and rock which hurled sharpened spikes at their enemies, like the thrusting horns of charging bull ceratopsians. The Algaroi of Nim-Roda sought out, trapped, killed and ate countless numbers of these animals and fed them to their nephaliim allies. For this reason Nim-Roda was called the "Great Hunter" before the Sa-Tan. His men sought to imitate the magnificence and match the boldness of these beasts within their humanity.

The Ceratopsia fought many wars with men across the earth. There was ceaseless war and armies continually rose and fell manipulated by the Twelve. In this way the Algaroi diminished the large herds of ceratopsians that grazed the earth. The large herds were no more and these great and majestic beasts passed from creation. It grieved God. Always the nephaliim were in the midst of the conspiracies. The Twelve fed the huge wars among men through their sons the nephals. War raged without respite under Al-Algar Nim-Roda's reign.

After Al-Algar Nim-Roda, in the south came Ammel-Uanna, and after him from the west came Ammel-Galanna. Both Ammel-Uanna and Ammel-Galanna built large empires of warring men. Like the Ceratopsia before them in the north, these men boasted in the strength and might of the great styracosaurs. The empire of Ammel-Uanna, and Ammel-Galanna after him, crafted for themselves jagged horns that they devised to wear upon themselves as savage armour. They built engines bristling with spikes and outward pointing horns and pikes. They speared and impaled all their enemies. Their culture celebrated pointed and thrusting things that did harm. Great festivals were held in which hundreds of victims were hurled onto forests of pointed stakes from lofty temples. Captured styracosaurs were penned and suffered greatly during their revelries. Their mighty men wore great frameworks of jagged spikes making it difficult to approach them; they armed themselves with long metal-pointed pikes, tapered to fine points which made them most effective when fighting men in numbers. Tribal emblems were painted on their faces and on their shields, on their engines, flags, on their homes and on hillsides; two large painted eyes rimmed by fearsome spikes. This became an emblem of fear and trepidation to all men residing in the hinterland of this loathsome empire. The spiked Styracs were a people continually at war.

Ammel-Uanna was a cruel man. He would take his enemies and sew them into the insides of slain beasts and leave them under the sun to perish. Or he would deliver them to his nephal overlord who would cook the beast with the men inside. It delighted his king to eat the beasts and find men inside and hear their cries while his meat was cooking.

In the generation of Du-Muzi—that is, the sixth generation—in the west and after him En-Meush-Um-Galanna in the east, a great people grew up under these kings and the nephaliim with them. These men were fleet of foot and swift, being a slight people. They contrived flying weapons and attacked their enemies from great distances. They would swoop in on running beasts which they had captured and trained. They built cunning propulsion systems and great clouds of needles and poisoned darts filled the skies. They wore huge feathered garments around their wastes and elaborate headdresses of bone and feather that trailed behind them and rattled as they travelled. These men adopted the raptor as their totem: the swift velocirators and oviraptors and eagles and hawks and running birds with their fearsome talons. This generation also built a great society that fashioned musical instruments from the bones of men and from horns and shells. They carved things of many materials which mimicked the lyrical calls of the raptors. They were a colorful people that danced and revelled with fire but were completely evil. They did terrible things to their enemies when they captured them.

Sa-Tan hated them on account of the music they made. Nephals came to steal their music, for hatred of the music of heaven burned in the Watchers' hearts. The Red Serpent sent a host of slave men and nephaliim, and they overwhelmed the Raptormen. There was great slaughter and hundreds of thousands of men died on the plains of PaZuZu. There was never such a calamitous massacre, even afterward in the days of men after the Waters, nor will there be again, except at the end. The battles of PaZuZu were so fierce that men became scarce in that place. After this great war, the nephaliim stayed many years consuming the bones of the dead that lay about after the great undoing of the Raptormen in their lands.

In the tenth generation, there arose a great king of men in the north called U-Bar-Tutu who was also called Zi-U-Sudra. He completely subdued the men of his generation and subsumed the cultures of the peoples of Ensi-Pazi-Anna in the east and Enme-Du-Ranki in the west. Zi-U-Sudra built a great amalgam culture of these eastern and western peoples. They became mighty in war, for U-Bar-Tutu was a knowledgeable man and cunning and he allied himself with the nephals of those parts.

In his time there was a great war. It began among the eastern peoples who fought their brothers in the west over mines and forests filled with fruit that ran between the two peoples between Onés and western Van. U-Bar-Tutu lived in the north in his city. He rose up against the Eastmen who were led by warrior chieftains. U-Bar-Tutu gathered to himself armies of Pazi-Anna, Onés and Du-Ranki and rolled out across the steppes in an ocean of spears, flags, wheeled carts, wagons and on platforms pulled by giant beasts. They came to the fruiting forest belt and built their camp villages in a huge arc facing the lands of the Eastmen.

War ensued and lasted many years. Killing was continual in the forest belt and on the plain. Nephaliim came against each other. Great battles took place, but men also pursued and killed each other in lonely and private places, in forests and on rock passes. North struck East and East struck North. All were full of fear and hatred. There was no peace anywhere, just darkness and war, smoke and ruin. The forests as far as Thogoth were laid waste. Smoke billowed up to God from the earth without ceasing in the time of U-Bar-Tutu.

After years of fighting, fed by the fertility of humanity, a conspiracy of Eastmen chieftains came together. Their lords devised a plan to overwhelm U-Bar-Tutu's armies. The chiefs decided to draw their armies across a vast green plain confronting them in the west. The nephals had created disease and bred this into a lowly forest people known as the Hemenoi, which means white and black. They were a people skilled in poisons and used long blowpipes, poisoned darts, and stabbing pikes. Over many days the eastern tribes dug holes and tunnels and the Hemenoi were sent into this place, a vast plain of pits where once there had been forests now destroyed by war. They concealed them, and there they lived like a subterranean race fed from above by the Eastmen while the war raged on.

When the time was right, the eastern tribes gathered all their armies together and prepared for a huge battle. Their drums and horns blew and fierce was their war cry. The armies of U-Bar-Tutu were lured into the eastern plains where the Hemenoi were concealed. As the battle raged, the eastern tribes held as the fighting swayed back and forth. Gradually they fell back and passed over the Hemenoi hidden in their holes and tunnels under the deforested plain.

In the early hours of daylight, mists rose up from the ground. War was engaged and there was terrific slaughter as men wrestled with each other across a massive front. Weapons clashed and blood flowed. Thousands of men died. The great war machines became worn from the continual hurling of rocks and the firing of bolts. As twilight fell, the great horns of all the tribes of the East were blown and the Eastmen fell back after a day of carnage. U-Bar-Tutu's armies came on enraged. The fighting West peoples crossed over and passed above the Hemenoi craftily concealed in their subterranean catacombs. The Hemenoi came up in the night, and passed among the ranks, carts, wagons, machines and warriors of the West. The Hemenoi, painted with mud and black and white paint poisoned the warriors of U-Bar-Tutu with their blowpipes and stabbing pikes. Even though they were slaughtered, their bodies spread the disease with which they were infected among the men of the West so that a great plague broke out. The western men could not rally against them as the Hemenoi spread out like water through the entire army and fell in their thousands at the hands of U-Bar-Tutu.

The Henemoi died in huge numbers, for they were lightly armoured, but not before they tore out the center of U-Bar-Tutu's armies like killing ghosts. They killed thousands and thousands of men this way. U-Bar-Tutu's mighty men became confused and scattered by the killings. The army became weakened and afraid on account of the plague that killed them. Then the Eastmen pressed back against them like a surging wave.

The East prevailed. U-bar-Tutu's armies broke and scattered. They fell apart and fled in all directions. The Eastmen were among them until a great ocean of humanity was killing and being killed across countless miles away back to the north and west of Pazi-Anna. The tribes of the East surged round and burned the empire of U-Bar-Tutu and destroyed everything of the West. They razed the cities of Onés, Eva and Pazi-Anna. Everywhere the nephaliim feasted and encouraged the slaughter.

The chief man U-Bar-Tutu took refuge in his capital city in the north and rallied his captains. They pressed men of Nod, Algaroi and Nimroda in the far north into service, and gathered thousands of warriors from the shores of the Sea of Nod. These men were skilled archers and were thrust in a line miles long in front of the city of U-Bar-Tutu. They shot every Hemenoi they spotted and brought them down amongst the ranks of the fighting men, where later they were all burned. U-Bar-Tutu held back the Eastmen and the bodies of the Hemenoi now polluted the armies of the East. Over many days the Hemenoi were thinned out. Then nepahaliim of CHaRuN came with fearsome weapons of sound and attacked the Eastmen slaughtering them back towards the east. The eastern tide was stemmed and a line of exhaustion was drawn as the war was fought to a standstill.

Eventually a travelling body of armoured nephaliim came from TaRTaRos that had followed the men of Algaroi and Nimroda south. They attacked the eastern tribes from behind through the great Forest of Thogoth. The fighting progressed many months. Men were scattered by the technologies and strength of these nephals, especially their weapons of sound. The Eastmen caught between U-Bar-Tutu and the nephaliim of TaRTaRos were smashed like soft metal between hammer and anvil. They were dispersed and hunted down and destroyed by nephaliim and men. Some escaped into the mountains that rimmed the land. The eastern armies were crushed masterfully by the nephals of TaRTaRoS. These god-men wore armour of bone and metal resembling the great beasts of the earth and were moulded into contorted faces of subjugated men. The nephaliim were skilled in spiritual devices and could bring up winds of confusion that bewildered warriors in battle. They then fell upon them and slew them amidst the wind and dust, plucking them up as they came among them swinging their hammers and scythes and fearsome cutting weapons, for they loved to draw blood. Some nephals preferred blunt things for pounding while others preferred sharp things for the killing of many quickly.

As well as using weapons of sound to drive men to their knees, the nephaliim also utilised weapons of concentrated light that blinded men and burned through them as they fought or fled. Nephaliim redirected rivers and spilled lakes to flood the armies of men so that they became mired. The nephals then waded through the mud and killed as many men as they could for they were no match for them mired in swamps and quagmires. After defeating their enemies, nephals would fall upon the camps and homes and despoil and ruin and torment the women and children of men; they then burned all their animals and everything that had resisted them. In this way the cities and lands of the Eastmen were undone.

These then were some of the great wars among men from the third to the tenth generations.

Several smaller armies and tribes of men existed in many places, such as the Ankylosoi, who fought with great clubs and bodies of spiked armour plating welded together with metals. They built strong fortresses in their mountain fastnesses, and wore helmets hard and steeled with savage crests and domes. Their soldiers were hard men and resisted many weapons. But they were subdued with nets and pits and flooded plains and other men devised ways to undo them.

There was also the Alsoi who in these times, were taught by the nephaliim to fly. Their flights were only ever devised as evil designs and the nephaliim used them to invade and overwhelm peoples otherwise hidden in valleys and vales. The Alsoi brought reports of things unknown to the nephaliim. The winds carried these men but they were shot down and captured. Rival nephaliim sought them out and destroyed the knowledge wherever it was found. In time only a few men flew such contrivances and eventually the knowledge passed away.

In other places where men were gathered together they fought back against the enclaves of the nephaliim and historic slaughters took place; they could not kill many of the nephaliim for they were cunning and steeped in knowledge. Men only were able to destroy the servants of the nephaliim in various places, and so men killed men.

Nephaliim and men adopted every design and culture inspired by their imagination. Their societies were cunningly evil, and always bent on war, killing, domination and the lust of power. Men were in mortal fear of roaming nephals, since they could do little to protect themselves from them. At times they fought hard against their oppression, but men were never free. There was no love; men perverted it with selfishness. Natural affection grew cold. They could not unite and work as brothers; instead they preyed upon each other. The nephaliim ruled over them and oppressed them with the object of destroying them altogether. Men were weak of soul, indulgent and looked only to the needs of the body.

Over all the evil, despair and destruction, the Fallen Ones rejoiced, especially Sa-Tan who was worshipped over all the earth with his consort and by the nephaliim and the men they enslaved.

Evil Men ruled in the earth alongside the nephaliim and were used by them and died in their vanity and arrogance by the evils they promulgated against others in the earth. They died by murders, and fire, and machines, and disease. They were the chief men after Oné and besides En-Ocha, Methu-Saleh and Nu who were not evil in their times and whom the nephaliim never corrupted in their years.

The earth groaned as the kings of men fought with each other and the nephaliim. And God was grieved.

> And graves have yawn'd, and yielded up their dead;
> Fierce fiery warriors fought upon the clouds,
> In ranks and squadrons and right form of war,
> ... The noise of battle hurtled in the air,
> Horses did neigh, and dying men did groan,
> And ghosts did shriek and squeal ...[1]
>
> There is a tide in the affairs of men,
> Which, taken at the flood, leads on to fortune;
> Omitted, all the voyage of their life
> Is bound in shallows and in miseries.[2]

---

1. William Shakespeare, *Calpurnia*.
2. William Shakespeare, *Brutus*.

During these eons Sa-Tan took the name of Baal, and received worship from nephaliim and all men. He was called also Baal-Zeebub, which means Lord of Flies, that is, Death, since his minions gathered over death and decay like flies on a corpse. The great Fallen One ABRaXaS set himself up as the consort of Baal and was worshipped as the great female goddess. This Watcher was also called Asatre, Aphrodite or the Ashtoreth in the tongues of men.

Wherever Baal set up his throne, things were detestable. The rituals were vile involving torment, death and pain. Dark evils shrouded the land and minds of men and nephals. Smoke rose ever from the throne of Sa-Tan and his dominion was blackened with blood and fire.

The nephaliim taught their women slaves all number of secrets from the heavenly knowledge of their fallen fathers. Women grew experienced in the knowledge of plants and roots, poisons and drinks. They learned about seeds that opened windows to the lower heavenly places. They poisoned each other, and drove others mad with the saps and juices of things, tormenting each other with spiritual weapons. The earth grew to be an exceedingly dark and evil place through vile religions of all conceivable darkness. These grotesque things are too black to describe even in this sacred writ.

God looked upon the earth and was grieved in his heart. He knew all that would come to pass, yet he despaired of the violence and continual evil that man chose. God grieved that he had ever made the earth. Yet still he waited.

In those days a mighty thing took place. Such was the grief of the earth, that the skins of the earth cracked and broke, and the land broke apart with earthquakes and deep sighs from deep within the ground. The bowels of creation sought to spew out of its mouth the evil Watchers and their spawn from off its skin. The table of the earth broke up and large portions began to drift asunder in those days. Seas opened up between the shores and the land that had been one, drifted apart beyond the Great Plain. The pieces of the great table of the earth drifted away from each other. The world was changed, but not so much as when the Waters of God came. However, huge tsunamis rolled in across the flat lands in various places and buried and drowned huge herds of animals and many men. They were all buried and given to the rocks.

Eventually the lands settled from their breaking and the waters of the deep settled and were contained. Nephaliim and beasts and birds of the air grew in these places and became different from each other; the great kingdoms of men under the nephaliim and orders of animals grew in variety and diversity. Yet many animals were extinguished altogether by the hunger and destruction of men and nephaliim, as were plants and trees of the fields. They were all cut down and great fires were burned for war.

Majestic sloths with shaggy and matted coats of fur hung in the colossal trees hundreds of feet in the air clinging to massive branches by their hooked claws. They never came to the ground but lived and birthed and died in the great canopies. Their droppings fell to the earth hundreds of feet below and fertilised the root systems of the great goliaths of the forest, the Tané Megaloi. In time these all were burned and consumed in the fires that the nephaliim created. The giant sloths would climb higher into the forest giants as the fires raced up the trunks until they were consumed. Their massive nests of branches and trees became fireballs in the treetops and all the babies were consumed as they were nursed. Whenever nephaliim cut down a mighty tree with metals and fires and a sloth was found to be among the canopy branches, the nephaliim raised it up and impaled it on spikes to mock the gentle tree dwellers and their offspring alike. They were burned alive and tormented with spears and burning prods as they twisted on the mighty spikes upon which they were lifted up. In this way, almost all of the giant tree sloths of the earth perished by fire.

The trees were cut down and burned to serve the nephaliim for the burning of men and animals and to create ash with which their high places were washed and painted as long as they inhabited those evil abodes. Forests retreated as an insatiable demand for wood to construct their contrivances, their buildings and the altars that they demanded for their vile religions in which men and beasts were consumed. The nephaliim rejoiced in suffering, hated life, and drew pleasure from torments because of the hunger that existed within them.

86　THE BLOODRED TREE

Fafnir-Amon

11

Andraemon and Fafnir-Amon

Death closes all: but something ere the end,
Some work of noble note, may yet be done,
Not unbecoming men that strove with gods.

—Tennyson, *Ulysses*

Outside in the distance a wildcat did growl
Two riders were approaching,
The wind began to howl.

—Bob Dylan, *All Along the Watchtower*

Before the birth of Nu, there was a great hunter in the earth before the LoGoi called Andraemon. He lived in the Myrrion, that is north GoRgoNos. Andraemon hated the evil and despair of men. There were not many nephaliim in that place, for none of the Watchers of the West—ZeMu, GoRgoNos or DRaKaVc—were Watchers of the Flesh, but disembodied spirits.

In the days of Du-Mazi, a time of the death of many men, the Great Mothers of Andraemon's people found their way by long and treacherous paths to a hidden vale surrounded by swamps. Andraemon was raised within the sheltered embrace of this sanctuary. During his youth he was told stories about Unos and the times before. He grew strong and bold, but was kept away from men until he was mature in years.

One day he ventured from the swamps of the Myrrion and made a long journey to the Great Plain to see the fires and smoke that burned in those places. By night he crept and using stealth, saw men, observed their evil practises and loathsome lives. He studied them like the hunter he was, concealed. One evening during a hunt, he saw some women attacked and taking up rocks he broke down upon the men. Andraemon slew five men. The women shrieked and sang and clung to him, and many others drew to him also, boys, and men. Andraemon drew them away from that place and brought them into the thickly wooded hills to the east.

Andraemon built a village and his people prospered. He went and visited the Great Mothers, but they would not come with him. They blessed him and withdrew into the fastnesses of the Myrrion, for they were afraid. He left them and returned to the hills and forests of Andraemon.

Andraemon taught all the children he had gathered about Unos; he also ensured they were fed and lived securely. His sons grew around him. Andraemon's spirit groaned within him for all the evil of men and the oppression of the nephaliim. In his grief he fashioned for himself a mighty bow of spliced woods. He soaked it in oils and honed and mastered the bow with skills given him by the LoGoi. Andraemon made great shafts to fire from his bow, and these he framed with the feathers of raptors and edged with iron points he cast from metals shown him by the Great Mothers.

No man could pull Andraemon's bow, for he was an extremely strong man. With these tools he became an even greater hunter, and fed his people. Andraemon protected his domain. He and his sons killed all evil men who drew near to their domain and in this way they protected their people. After many years, his people saw their first nephal up close. Its name was Fafnir-Amon. It was a large hideous creature resembling a man with a crooked back, massive legs and a contorted face with large protruding teeth and blunted bone growths protruding from its forehead. Bony outgrowths also protruded down the spine of its back. Fafnir-Amon had three huge fingers on his left hand and a blooded stump on his right to which he had fastened an ugly hook and cutting spear. He could not feed himself unless falling upon carcasses and tearing at flesh with his teeth. He was covered in large sores that seeped and were rank; nevertheless, he was strong and hard. Trailing from his waist were long chains from which hung living and dead slaves that Fafnir-Amon fed off while he walked. This wretched caravan was dragged wherever he went, as far as they could travel and when one died, their bodies were dragged about or tossed in fires and eaten by the creature and those chained to him. Fafnir-Amon would grab people in raids and chain them to his body like a mobile larder. Once captured, no man escaped Fafnir. They lived and died tied to the terrible creature. Their living terror, despair and exhaustion was continual and they were forced to devour the dead among them, only to be consumed themselves. In this way the hapless victims were dragged to and fro across the land.

Fafnir's legs were powerful muscular trunks that terminated in distorted clumps of calloused flesh and bone. His skin was grey and mottled and pockmarked with white sores seeping pus. Vile black blood left stains over his hardened skin. He wore iron armour that he had fashioned from his skills in metallurgy. He had a massive protruding enlarged eye, and two smaller eyes on the sides of his large hairless skull that allowed him to see in different directions. He roared like a beast and beat the earth in his hunger. His hulk smelt rank, like rotting flesh in stagnant water.

As a child, Andraemon had heard of the nephaliim in the stories told him as a child around the campfires of the Myrrion. One evening, while on a camp on the outskirts of his domain, some of his scouts heard the roar and bellowing of the creature in the distance and ran toward the oncoming retinue on the outskirts of their land. Andraemon moved his people into a hidden place deep in the Myrrion, and then tracked Fafnir-Amon within the interior learning the creature's ways.

Andraemon was keen of sight and skilled in concealment. He wore clothes and hard papers made of blended plant materials and textiles woven from the hides of creatures. He was more skilled than any man at traversing forest and rock and could climb and run and was agile in treetops. On his chest he wore large metal bosses held by straps that crossed his chest and back in broad Xs emblazoned with an insignia of Unos taught him by the Mothers. The sign was an upturned man reaching toward the earth with outstretched arms.

As he tracked the creature and observed the misery of his fellow men, Andraemon decided to kill the great beast that had come into his land. He prepared great bolts of the hardest woods, which he soaked and crafted and fitted with the finest raptor feathers. Andraemon tested these over and over until he had a fine quiver full of straight and true bolts tuned harmoniously to the great spliced bow. He trained his sons and his sons' sons and together they crafted many arrows. Andraemon carried his great bow across his body, secured by the metal bosses of

Unos. His hair was brown and he wore it short and had his women cut it, so that he was unlike others, for men in those days rarely cut their hair but wore it in wild tangled tresses.

After many days of tracking and observing Fafnir-Amon, Andraemon travelled to a large water hole where the creature liked to lay and drink and cake itself in mud to fight off the bitting flies of the plain, the painful zebubas and the boring parasites known as eduli.

Fafnir-Amon and his chained slaves came down to the water and the creature unshackled himself and got down on all fours and gulped up water like a ceratopsian. Andraemon and his sons lay concealed. Then the great hunter ran around the circle of the pond. Taking a long metal wire with savage serrations that he had concealed in the grass, he ran courageously toward the nephal. Running quickly through the chattering and howling human creatures bound to Fafnir-Amon's chains, Andraemon wound the wire around one of the great creature's ankles and leapt back into the grass. While Fafnir-Amon gathered himself up from the mud, Andraemon drove the serrated wire deep into the ground with a spike and hammered it down with a heavy rock. As Fafnir-Amon rose, the serrations cut into his flesh. In a rage the creature roared, tore the spike from the ground and flailed the wire through the grass. Fafnir-Amon began to run. He was not fast but was large and could cover ground quickly. The serrations however got the better of him and cut his ankle to the bone slowing his dash. Andraemon was gone, leaping through the marshy reeds around the pond. As the nephal flattened the marshes, Andraemon took two long bolts and strung them to his bow. Pulling back with all his strength he aimed them at Fafnir-Amon and fired.

The bolts sped, but the creature saw them coming with his side eyes and dodged. One flew into the marsh behind; the other shot through one of the chained slaves passing clear through his torso and pinning him to the ground several hundred feet behind the great creature. The cluster of slaves screamed but the tangled chains around their necks held them in a cluster where they were: men, women, children and several dirty corpses in varying stages of decay. Fafnir-Amon was enraged and drew two savage throwing weapons from his belt and hurled them in the direction of where the arrows had come. The scything disks with three large metal-edged claws cut through the marsh stems and dropped into the muddy waters beyond Andraemon who was already running.

Fafnir took a small metallic whistle from his war pouch and blew into it. The scythes picked up the harmonic and echoed back revealing their location in the mud. The sons of Andraemon now arose from grasses on the other side and fired a hail of arrows into the people and the raging nephal. The men were cut down and pinned to the ground, but the arrows would not penetrate Fafnir-Amon's hide or his armour.

The nephal crouched down and leapt high into the air to see above the reeds. He took an instrument clipped to the belt that circled his waist and pushed the two sharp prongs along one edge into his left temple. This actuated his heat senses and he now closed his eyes and scanned the horizon from where he had come. He could clearly make out the small army of men in the marshes, his dead and dying chained larder, and a single man concealed in a tall tree at the head of the water hole watching him.

He un-wrapped the wire entrenched tightly around his ankle flesh, and circled in a slow arc around to the west, closing in towards the men concealed in the marshes. Andraemon observed him from his tall tree and whistled raptor-fashion to his men who quickly dispersed to the east and west of the waterhole. Fafnir-Amon observed them all as heat patterns in his head and changed course now running in a loping roll toward the men armed with bows and pikes.

Andraemon called to them, but Fafnir-Amon closed quickly and they were caught against the marshy water of the pond. The great nephal came crashing through the low scrub, frothing and bellowing, with hideous war shrieks that sent the men into a terrified panic. The outer Andraemonoi lifted their pikes but the nephal crashed upon them like a wave, swinging his fearsome weapon and the scything hook and spear bound to his arm. The Andraemonoi were utterly undone, bodies, limbs and flesh flying in all directions as the beast fell among them—biting, slashing and crushing. Blood splattered all over the creature as he shrieked and gibbered in an insane orgy of exultation.

Andraemon screamed as his sons and grandsons went down, crushed under Fafnir-Amon's feet, slashed and dismembered by his fearsome weapons. Fafnir screamed with joy, his eyes bulging, as he bit and mouthed his victims in a frenzy of blood lust and excitement.

Andraemon and the western cluster of archers and pikemen withdrew, wailing and weeping for their brothers as they set off at a run.

Fafnir-Amon stayed at the mud hole all that evening and into the night, eating the dead and smashing their bodies and limbs against the ground to break open their bones so he could suck the blood and soft flesh from their ruined bodies.

Deep in the night Andraemon and his sons reached their village with the exultant bellowing of the nephal coursing in the distance across the still evening air. The Andraemonoi hastened the women and children together and Andraemon sent them deeper in to the Myrrion to the Great Mothers with his most trusted warriors. The rest sat in the dust around their empty homes and wept and threw dust on their heads.

As the sun dawned, Andraemon and his sons were up early. Grim faced and covered in dust, with long streaks etched down their bodies by tears, they gathered all their weapons together. Andraemon had not expected his arrows to bounce off the hardened hide of the creature. They talked together and made a plan.

Fafnir-Amon also arose with the dawn. He hauled himself from the mud, belched, and coughed great gobbets of human flesh and bone from his massive gullet. Bending down he sniffed the ground and, standing, roared out a challenge to the men who had eluded him and massacred his larder. He let out a contemptuous laugh at the man of the tree and bellowed boastfully in his tongue how much he had enjoyed destroying the sons of the tree man, how flavourful they were to him and how they now filled his belly. Fafnir-Amon then began a sweep of the land in the direction his prey had escaped the day before, slowly and meticulously tracking the heat traces still left on the ground and through the reeds from the evening before.

The Andraemonoi had already circled in a wide arc several miles to the north and come around towards the water hole from a new approach. Andraemon climbed high into the canopy near the water hole but they could not see the nephal. His tracks were clear however and the men tracked him some miles towards the north.

Andraemon called to Fafnir-Amon and challenged him. In response the creature turned and laughed a deep cruel laugh while fingering the severed limbs of man-prey stuffed into the wide war belt fastened about his stomach.

The nephal came on. Andraemon stood his ground with great courage for a charging nephal was a terrible sight to behold. The man braced his feet firmly and, with controlled breaths, fixed a favourite bolt to his bow and pulled the string back. The string wined as it was tensed and Andraemon heard it sing next to his ear. The nephal was now roaring and thundering towards the man less than 400 hundred feet away. Foam trailed from his vulgar mouth as a long stretched ribbon until it broke apart and fell in heavy blotches to the dust churned up by his smashing feet.

Andraemon breathed slowly and deeply as the terrible foe crashed toward him. He gathered all his courage and, aiming at Fafnir's largest eye, let his bolt fly. It came straight and true, but hit Fafnir-Amon above the eye and glanced off his brow clattering harmlessly to the ground. Andraemon dropped a second shafted bolt from his teeth and caught it in his hand. With a swift and efficient motion it was swept up, and fitted to his bow. Fafnir-Amon was now within one hundred feet. The ground shook. The leaves on the nearest trees trembled and the thundering vibrations went up through Andraemon's legs and caught in his throat as panic began to creep over his entire frame as the roaring behemoth came on.

He calmly released the second bolt. It sped and crashed deep into Fafnir-Amon's large central eye. Andraemon immediately dropped to the side, rolled, and then jumped to his feet and ran as fast as his legs would carry him, his muscles screaming. Water, blood and pus gushed from the sloshing hole wrapped around the shaft of Andraemon's bolt. Fafnir-Amon roared with rage and anger, sweeping forward with his hook. But he was not down. With his side eyes he saw Andraemon's flight. He raced after his prey and followed the running man with great loping strides, the shaft of Andraemon's arrow still hanging from the oracle in the centre of his head. A long stream of discolored fluid painted a bloody bib down the front of the nephal. He began to close on the agile fleeing man, swaying his head from side to side so he could focus with his side eyes on the fleeing prey. As he closed, he drew his large metallic weapon ready to strike.

Fafnir-Amon came on in vengeance and fury, smashing the trees and branches away with his jagged sword. Andraemon ran, and agilely swung up into the trees. Running up a snaking branch several feet thick, he disappeared in to the green embrace of the tall canopy. Fafnir-Amon came ragging past scything through the grasses and trees. Andraemon sat silently above, watching as the creature passed below. But Fafnir-Amon stopped, turned and looked up into the tree at the man. He laughed.

"I shall have thee raw and after plucking your limbs you will watch me burn and eat all thy sons. Some I shall roast alive, others I will torment on spikes as you sit there, a bleeding torso. You shall all be food for Fafnir, your sons, your women, your children, your beasts and everything of you. I, Fafnir-Amon will have you!"

he said in the common tongue as he slavered and cackled up at Andraemon in the canopy. Fafnir-Amon took burning embers from a metallic firebox that opened as a lid on one of the bosses of his breast plate, and blew on them. Thrusting them into a pile of brush they crackled through the dry leaves. The grass immediately ignited. Fanning it with sweeps of his huge weapon, the flames took and began to flourish amongst the brush around the trees.

Andraemon swung up and climbed away across the canopies until he was upwind of the smoke. The nephal took the fire and spread it through the underbrush until a great conflagration was encouraged. He burned everything around and ran to and fro seeking Andraemon. But Andraemon was already more than half a mile distant where he came to his men who had gathered at a pre-arranged place. They gathered on a narrow dirt trail between mighty trees latticed by large thorned bushes. Days earlier the men had prepared a deep pit. Large wooden spikes were sunk deep into its base. The site had been chosen well. The path ran in a curve between dense strong trees and high banks of creeping thorns. The men prepared their bows and Andraemon blew his horn. Fafnir-Amon heard the sound and came charging with great vengeance.

The men revealed themselves as the creature closed in on them and loosed bolts off at him at will, which simply enraged the nephal and quickened his lumbering run toward the small body of warriors. His bony stumps pounded across the plain through the fire and smoke. Andraemon loosed off a bolt that hit the nephal in the crotch but did not penetrate. The fearsome beast came crashing through the undergrowth toward them, swinging his sword and hook. 400 hundred feet, 300 feet, 200 hundred feet . . . arrows pelted across his breastplate. Andraemon shouted to his sons and stirred their courage, for they had never faced a foe like this at such close range—100 feet. In front of them lay the carefully concealed pit with its frightful spikes. Although blind with rage and anger, Fafnir was no fool. He detected the surface of the path, saw how branches, foliage and sand had been spread across only a portion of the path. Bellowing, he leapt up and soared over the disturbed ground and landed barely ten feet short of the Andraemonoi. They scattered to the sides like flies and Andraemon turned and began to run back down the edge of the curving path away from the laughing nephal directly behind him.

And this was the beast's great undoing. As he lumbered forward the ground gave way and Fafnir-Amon crashed down into Andraemon's masterfully prepared second pit on which his sons had stood atop large pole heads interspersed throughout the pit. The surface was laced with wattle and branches and covered with large leaves and then compacted sand. The disturbed ground ahead of it had been a ruse, made to appear like a concealed pit, over which Fafnir had instinctively leapt only to crash more violently into the real trap just a few paces on.

The nephal landed heavily in the bottom, his full weight pressing him down. Jagged stout posts with honed points thrusting up through his gut, underbelly, feet and crotch. His great weight, the force of his leap, and the few forward staggers on the path drove him downward onto Andraemon's spikes that hungrily bit into the great descending hulk. Fafnir-Amon's black blood came gushing out and splattered around the walls of the pit. He let out a terrible gut-wrenching scream of agony, anger and contempt as the spikes thrusting through his pelvis, legs and lower back. But he was not dead yet. The nephaliim were hardy and strong and Fafnir-Amon was still deadly.

Swirling his great hook around the lip of the pit he collected one of the Andraemonoi and the screaming man fell back into the pit where the nephal smashed him to pulp with the end of his fist. Andraemon had planned well, however, and even as the nephal struggled, he and his sons took embers already burning in metal bowls nearby. Wrapping them in straw gathered in small piles around the bowls, they tossed them down into the pit which was floored with a deep pillow of dry grasses and straw.

The fire caught and hungrily licked up as Fafnir-Amon struggled to lift his lower body off the spikes, pieces of human still hanging in strips from his jagged hook. But the Andraemonoi had serrated the posts with saws and hammered downward-slanting pins into the shafts of the stakes. The serrations tore through muscle and soft flesh and the pins locked deep within the nephals muscle and tissue, holding him fast. Fafnir-Amon pounded the fire with his weapon, still in hand, but this only scattered the burning grasses and fuelled the blanket of flame now wrapping itself closely around his flesh.

Andraemon drew a bolt and at close range fired it into the nephal's second eye and then another into his third eye so that Fafnir-Amon's world went black. The great creature was not done yet. It urinated and vomited forth its bile and extinguished much of the flame. The Andraemonoi then took huge spears that they had carefully laid in the thickets around the pit and with all their might, drove them down into the nephal. They broke off as the creature wrestled back and forth firmly held in the pit, the broken shafts lolling about like the spines of a giant porcupine. The men then rolled a large ball of brush, grass, wood and bark in over the top of Fafnir-Amon, and poured pitch down on top of the creature. It immediately caught fire and engulfed the nephal in a cloak of fiery agony as his armour heated and seared into his flesh and the oily flames licked down his ungodly frame. His lungs filled with acrid smoke as he panted and bellowed, cursing and blaspheming with every vile rebuke he could conceive. Andraemon's warriors had painted the walls of the pit with tar, and this too now caught fire, so the creature was fixed in a bowl of consuming flame.

Andraemon took to the trees above the pit and began firing his carefully prepared bolts into Fafnir-Amon's flesh as he struggled to tear off his armour as the fire cooked him. Eventually the smoke, fire, the spikes from below and the pikes driven in from above overwhelmed Fafnir-Amon. His great teeth bit at the wall of the pit. There was a loud and bellowing scream that dissipated into a long deep groaning and then finally the creature's head and shoulders slumped forward and the jagged weapon fell from his hand. The flames licked up and the smoke thickened. The Andraemonoi drew back, knowing it was done.

> Can it be any but some monstrous god of evil
> That has sent this doom upon me?[1]

> ... he puts alms for oblivion,
> A great-sized monster of ingratitudes:
> Those scraps are good deeds past;
> Which are devour'd
> As fast as they are made, forgot as soon
> As done ... [2]

1. Sophocles, *Antigone*.
2. William Shakespeare, *Ulysses*.

As the smoke rose, the Andraemonoi trailed off towards the Myrrion in the south but Andraemon stayed until the fire burned low and the bones and wreckage of his adversary were a smoking ruin. He stayed all night, talking to God and then he walked wearily to the south after his kin, until the hills of the Myrrion enfolded him. It had been a day of men.

Andraemon was the first man to kill a nephal in a duel and ever afterward his people praised him in song. The nephal and his ruined slaves were no more. The Andraemonoi came in later days and filled in the hole, and Fafnir-Amon passed beyond memory. The chains and weapons and accoutrement of Fafnir's retinue, along with his hapless victims, were buried and burned by Andraemon and his people in the pit, but the destroyed Andraemonoi were respectfully gathered together and carried away to the Myrrion.

The people lived in peace for a generation. It was many years before nephaliim came again into the Myrrion, but come they did.

12

Nu of Van

As surely as I live, declares the Sovereign LORD,
Even if Noah, Daniel and Job (lived in those times),
They could save neither son nor daughter.
They would save only themselves.

—Ezekiel 14:20

The storm god charged the land like a bull
[on the rampage].
He smashed [the earth] in pieces [like a clay pot]
The gale, the Flood, it flattened the land.

—The Epic of Gilgamesh 106–29, tablet XI.

船八

— "Vessel," "eight" (ancient Chinese)

In isolated places rimmed by mountains and high passes God had a remnant of the children of Oné who still loved him and were kept from the seed of Shemgazi and the curse of the nephaliim.

Far to the east of Onés, north of where Phirst had been, in a valley on a high plateau, a man named En-Ocha was born. As a child he yearned to know of Unos. He spent many days with the great father Oné and the great mother Eva talking with them and discussing the details of the things that had been before, things that occurred before his great grandparents died and were given to the rivers of fire west of Phirst. En-Ocha learned the way of things and became very wise. He called upon the name of Unos and was faithful in the annual fire offerings of the land to God. Unos drew near and visited him in his dreams. There were visions of what had been and what was still to come. En-Ocha taught all his children and their children these wondrous things and this greatly pleased God. Men round about feared En-Ocha as a great seer and a wise man, and God kept him away from the nephaliim and out of their knowledge up on the high plateau where Phirst had been. The people of En-Ocha near Phirst prospered as men had done in the earliest days.

In time all the Phirst men of old and their wives grew old and died. Oné lived 963 years and was buried by his sons in the cracks of Phirst where the fire of the veins of the earth could be seen. The flames under the earth consumed Oné's body. Eva too was burned in the rivers of fire. The people of Phirst carried their bodies away to the fire cracks in great ceremony, Oné first and then Eva. On the day each died, the cleft of the distant mountains against which the sun dropped, was noted and huge standing stones aligned with the mark by the people. Here the people stayed, and for a whole year mourning and celebration continued until the sun came round again and dropped once more behind the cleft of the mountains marking the day of their parting. But afterwards men buried their fathers in caves or in the ground where they heaped up high mounds of dirt over them. But the nephaliim would come and dig out the men and eat their bones.

En-Ocha had a son. On the day he was born, God appeared to En-Ocha and told him he would judge the nephaliim and all evil men; that he would be gracious and wait unless even one man turned and called on the name of Unos.

"Across the span of thy son's time I wait, but when he dies, judgement will come. As his lifeblood plays out so I will play blood out upon the earth from above. Waters of cleansing will come and the earth will be cleaned, for I am sorely grieved that I made man and of the pollution of the earth by the evil ones."

En-Ocha's son was therefore called Methu-Saleh, which means, "While I live the waters shall not come." He was a watchword and a warning that God intended to wash the whole earth with a great judgement. So great was God's grace in the face of so much evil and the provocation of men and the corruption of all flesh by the Watchers and their vile offspring the nephaliim, that Methu-Saleh lived the longest of any man upon the earth. His life was 987 years.

When Methu-Saleh was very old, and after Oné's death, Great God said to Unos that man would no longer live forever, but his years on the earth would be one hundred and twenty, ten times the number of the Twelve. And God set one hundred and twenty years for man's earthly existence, and one hundred and twenty years till the coming of his great judgment to shorten all troubles.

After Methu-Saleh, there came Lam-Ech, and to Lam-Ech came Nu. He was called Nu by En-Ocha, for his great grandfather knew it would be in his generation that God's cleansing would come. Nu means "cease from labours." En-Ocha, Methu-Saleh, Lam-Ech and Nu lived in the mountains on a raised plateau above the plain of Shinar northwest of Phirst. Lam-Ech, however, was an evil man and he departed and dwelt at the foot of the mountains.

Nu walked with his great grandfather and went up to him in the heights and talked of many things, of the angels and the heavens and the earth and of Unos and the ways of God. It was from En-Ocha and Methu-Saleh his fathers that Nu learned of the great water judgement to come.

The numerous evils on the earth grieved God, but in the mountain fastnesses above Shinar, Nu and his family and the descendents of En-Ocha served God and offered the annual festival gifts. En-Ocha walked with God and Unos came to him as he had Oné. En-Ocha was greatly beloved so he was taken away to the lowest heaven and he did not return to men.

Before he was taken away, Unos showed En-Ocha many things, secrets about the future as well as truths from the first days. En-Ocha had developed writing and ways of conveying things in signs and symbols to his people. The family of En-Ocha were the inventors of writing but afterward many other peoples learned the skills.

En-Ocha wrote on parchments he made but towards his final year, and sensing his time was shortened on the earth, he cast a mighty pillar of gold. On it he inscribed all the truths of things he had known and he set the pillar up in a high place. Then he carved into wet bricks of clay the same truths and he baked these so they became hard. He set the bricks into a mighty round tower and assembled them at the foot of the mountains. Men came and wondered at the pillars of writing. Some foolishly worshipped the pillars, especially the gold one in the heights, which they called "Father the Sun;" the brick tower they called "Mother the Moon." But En-Ocha drove them off. Nu came to read and have explained the truths of the pillars of En-Ocha.

The two pillars were beacons. En-Ocha set them up as a testimony to men, as a record to survive as a testimony after the cleansing that he knew would come. But God broke them down and cast them away in the great tumult of judgement, because they had become things of worship, least afterward men turned to them again and worshipped them as gods. After En-Ocha was taken, his sons searched and searched for him, even though their father had told them his time had come and he would not be found. But Nu went to the pillars, and carefully studied the words on them that his great-grandfather had made. He took the wondrous book his great-grandfather had cast in metal–365 pages, one for each year–and he wrote down all the things En-Ocha had recorded on the two ancient pillars. To En-Ocha's prophesys and insights he added information about his own times, and he kept the book in a special place, reading it regularly to his sons and their wives.

One evening in his 500th year, Nu lay in his stone and chalk house by the fire with his wife. He was an unusual man in having a single wife. The fire glinted against the brushed stonewalls of their home. As he watched the flickering light, the shapes took form and the form of a man appeared. Nu knew this was Unos of whom he had been taught and he rose and worshipped. The light left the wall and went before him and led him out from the house and into the fields under the firmament of despoiled teraphim and there Unos spoke with Nu in a vision of lights.

He instructed him to build a large ship in which he would save Nu and all the creatures of the earth that still remained. He showed Nu the way of the ship, and how to build it and make it strong. He showed him how to draw lines and plans and these he drew in lights in front of Nu who carefully studied everything he was told. Unos said he would send mighty cleansing waters on the earth in the year his grandfather Methu-Saleh died. Within one hundred and twenty years this would come to pass.

Nu drew up plans with his sons, Jahf, Sem and Hamaa. The men devised a method of casting wood in various shapes by scraping and chopping and casting it in moulds with resins as Unos had shown Nu, so that it set fast and bound stronger than any wood of a tree. They called it "gopha" which means "fluid" and "holds fast." Of gopha they constructed large pieces of wood of all shapes and complexities in mounds of clay upon the ground, and with these they constructed the ship that Unos had shown Nu. They fitted the pieces with hammered dowels and metal plugs. The joints they sealed with more gopha. With these pieces they began to construct the massive ship, set upon a huge framework. It was rounded at the bottom and flat on top, 300 arms long, thirty arms high and thirty arms wide in the measurements of the time. It took many decades, but the sons of Nu trusted their father and the vision he had with Unos. They built the great ship and it was their life.

Nu was a very tall man and he had large hands that were cut and callused from his labour. His skin was grey and he had long white hair, like a sheep, but he cut his beard during the years of the making of the ship. He wore a tunic of soft animal hide chewed subtle by his wife Nu-Anna. A strong belt of pliable metal clasped around his waist like a giant pincer. Above his waist he wore nothing when he worked on the ship.

When the family went out, they took pairs of huge dogs with them, as large as oxen. These creatures roamed about the Nu-oi in a protective cover. They were fearsome beasts to confront, but loved Nu and his sons, and warned Nu of evils that approached. They drove men and predatory wild animals away. The people were fearful of the Nu-oi on account of the dogs and because the family seemed to be able to speak to the animals and creatures came to them in peace. The people thought the Nu-oi were gods. They were afraid to stretch out their hands and harm them or ambush them. The dogs never allowed evil men to get near, and so Nu and his sons moved about the valley and worked in peace while the dogs protected them. The dogs were called the Nu-mastafoi, fast of foot and strong of jaw. They were keen of sight, ear and smell. They had beautiful stripes and mottled spots down their shaggy sides and sang with beautiful sounds and called to each other. They had strong necks and muscular forefronts tapering back to a lean pair of legs down their slanting back. Nu fed them the flesh of animals that died and on a mash made of nuts and fruits that he harvested. It was baked into a hard crust that the Nu-mastafoi chewed. Nu ground this food into a gruel that Nu-Anna and her daughters baked and fed to the Nu-mastafoi who had no need to hunt in the forests. These marvellous creatures lived to protect the family of Nu. When roused they were fearsome and could run long distances. They were tenacious and fearless. Some died in conflicts with greater animals and against men who on occasions trapped and killed them, which grieved Nu and his sons. The Nu-mastafoi were their most beloved creatures. The creatures were affectionate and faithful to Nu and his family. In the end, Nu took all that remained with him into the ship. The Nu-mastafoi were spared the waters because of their faithfulness to Nu. But their wild brothers were all destroyed.

In the seventh seasons when he travelled among men with the Nu-mastafoi at his side, he wore his glorious cloak made by Nu-Anna and his sons' wives. He had shoes of auroch hide, toughened in urine, and soft leaves and grasses were daily stuffed into his shoes by his loving wife, so that his feet were not chaffed.

His eldest son Jahf was not as tall as his father, and his skin was white, not grey. His hair was blond–which greatly pleased his father–and his eyes were blue, the glory of his mother, who had azure eyes.

Hamaa was the tallest of the four, taller even than Nu. He had black skin, like jasper, and beaded hair. He had long gracious limbs and climbed nimbly through the high beams of the ship as it was raised to the sky. He had beautiful teeth and dark eyes, like coals, the most gracious of Nu's sons, like a gazelle.

Sem was a ruddy color, handsome, with black hair. He was the shortest of the sons but stocky and strong, with beautiful fingers. He wore no shoes, preferring to go barefoot so the soles of his feet were hard and calloused like that of a beast.

Jahf was the yolk of an egg, Hamaa was a black gazelle, Sem was a rock. Together they worked with their grey-skinned father with his white hair that hung down onto his shoulders, and his strong chin that hutted out beneath his bristling white beard.

Within the first year the four men, supported by their wives, marked out the circumference of the ship upon a plain, near to deep forests from which they shaved and cut the wood that they blended with the sap of resinous trees. White Jahf and black Hamaa took responsibility for raising the great skeleton that was the frame of the ship, and Sem, the ruddy-skinned rock, constructed plans for the making of the woods and their moulds, and drawings of the pens and stories that Unos had commanded Nu to build inside the great ship.

Nu oversaw all the details and corrected and guided the men, supervising all the work so that it was as he had been shown with the lights of Unos. Within the third year, the spine of the ship was made and its great ribs began to soar upward. They arched out like giant fingers grasping at the sky from the ground. Birds came and flew among the fingers and mighty pterasaurs flew down and inspected the great work. Sem was very skilful and completed detailed maquettes of the interior of the ship. He made these with fine tools he cast in metal parts and combined with fine wood and resin. Their wives drew up lists on parchments of all the animals that would be housed within the great ship as Unos had instructed. It was also in this year, that peoples began to drift up into the remote mountains above Shinar near Van. They were refugees who fled from the Great Plain below and the continual wars and terror of the nephaliim.

The people in the valley of Nu were evil and afraid. They mocked Nu but never came near, for they feared him and the great wooden fingers from the ground. They had heard of his great grandfather En-Ocha who was renowned and mighty. They thought Nu a god fearing he might fall upon them even as the nephaliim did. So the people inhabited the land around about, and hid in the deep forests around the plain where Nu and his sons built the great ship. But the men of the valley left the builders alone.

Every seventh year, Nu went out to the people. He travelled into the forests and God protected him. Nu spoke to the peoples of all the things he had learned from his fathers Methu-Saleh and En-Ocha and from the golden and baked-clay obelisks. But the people did not believe him. They were afraid and mocked Nu. For one hundred and twenty years Nu ministered to the peoples of the valleys and forests of his region while Jahf, Sem and Hamaa built up the great ship under their father's instruction according to the lights he had seen.

Nu grew very weary of his ministry. He despaired that none of the people took heed of why he built the great ship. Neither did they listen to Methu-Saleh who reproved the people on account of Lam-Ech who mocked the work of his kin. They neglected the great annual offering ceremonies when the family of Nu offered to God their gifts. From this time their offerings were consumed by fire as they had been in the days of Kainos. This amazed the peoples, and they thought the family of Nu gods, but they were marked for judgement. Their hearts and minds were never toward God, but always planning evil.

Nu and his family and the people thereabouts lived in a tense and isolated balance. The people did terrible things to the animals of the forests. They killed each other, and ate each other, but always were afraid of Nu and none came near to his place or interfered with the work of the great ship.

Nu had taken to himself a single wife, who was called Nu-Anna. She was a beautiful woman, with golden hair, white skin and azure-colored eyes. She grew her hair long and braided it about her body as a garment. Nu-Anna had intricate tattoos over her forehead and lower arms, above the wrists, as was the custom of her clan. Her marks were flowing curves, of vines and flowers and beautiful things. The pictures pleased Nu who loved such things. She was very wise and had a beautiful voice. Nu-Anna loved Nu and was ever at his side, except during the sixty-six-day-travelling season every seventh year, when Nu went out to the people with words. When he departed with the Nu-mastafoi, she sat by the great ship aching for his return and singing the ancient songs of healing, protection and comfort.

It was the custom in those days for wives to take as their first name the name of their husband. Anna was a grand-daughter of En-Ocha. As well as their first three sons, Nu and Nu-Anna had many other sons and many fair daughters, white, black and ruddy. Jahf and Hamaa took wives from among their sisters and had many offspring. But all the children of Jahf and Hamaa and the daughters of Nu abandoned the work of the great ship and wandered away into the forests and valleys after their own whims. They too grew evil among the other peoples and abandoned the annual offering and thought no more of Unos. They ate of the fruits and meats of the forest and wandered aimless through the years of their days beautiful, but lost in distraction and foolishness. This grieved Hamaa and Jahf and Nu and his wife, so that they stopped having children.

Sem did not take a wife from among his sisters, as was the custom. Instead, as he wandered in the forests gathering the resins and woods for the moulds and conceiving designs for the interiors of the great ship, he came across a hill top amidst the inner forest on the western border of the valley of Van. Here were hung on great spikes, a forest of children, pierced through with many wounds and partially burned with fire. Sem found among the many dead one alive, a girl, who was spiked through her left shoulder but who lived.

She was red, of the tribe of Kainos. Tattooed over her upper body and legs were fearsome images and cuts; of bloody beasts, snarling mouths and teeth, as was the custom of the Kainoi. She had red hair, matted with blood and dirt and her teeth were rasped to pointed fangs for the tearing of meat.

Sem cut the pole down, and carefully dis-impaled the child, and nursed her with waters and herbs that he had learned from his mother Nu-Anna. Sem gathered her up on a pole bed and dragged her back to the ship, tied to one of the Nu-mastafoi. His mother Nu-Anna nursed the child back to health, and taught her the ancient tongue and educated her in all the ways of Nu and his family. Sem took her as his wife when she was well. But he did not lay with her, out of respect for the great physical sufferings she had endured at the hands of evil men on the forest hill. The two were great friends and companions. They slept side by side and held each other, but were never man and woman together. Sem loved his wife whom he called Sem-Anna-Hill-Ashak, which means "woman of Sem who was dis-impaled from the hill." She joined the wives of Nu and Jahf and Hamaa and was happy and good. This was a grace from God in those days. Afterward, when the great waters abated, Sem-Anna-Hill-Ashak did lay with her husband, and they brought forth many children and prospered greatly, but not until after the Waters.

Besides Nu-Anna, wife of Nu, and Sem-Anna-Hill-Ashak, wife of Sem, the wives of Jahf were:

Jahf-Sumanna,
Jahf-Azmollec-Un-Anna (called Jahf-Anna),
Solmantaloc-Jahf and
Hill-Anna-Umaduzi-Jahf-Um.
The wives of Hamaa were:
Hamaaa-Umzalloch,
Anna-Numanna-Ham,
Hamaa-Oz-Olloc and
Hilluma-Ham.

But only Jahf-Anna and Hamaa-Oz-Olloc stayed with their husbands and continued to build the great ship. When the Waters came, only these were saved of the wives of Jahf and Hamaa. Their other sisters departed into the forests after their children, for they tired of the great work and were unfaithful to Nu and Nu-Anna, their husbands, and paid no mind to the stories of Unos or the annual offerings.

Only these eight were saved:
Nu and Nu-Anna,
Jahf and Jahf-Anna,
Hamaa and Hamaa-Oz-Olloc, and

Sem and his wife Sem-Anna-Hill-Ashak,

four men and four women, eight in all. They were a redemptive sign, unlike the eight generations of evil kings in the years after Oné and Kainos.

They were the only souls of men in all those days that restrained themselves from vice and futility, and the only people un-polluted by the Fallen Ones or nephaliim. All their other children died along with all other living things. Only eight survived, for they were pure of seed and heart and listened to Unos and trusted God as Methu-Saleh and En-Ocha had done before them.

But in the tenth year of the building of the ship, the nephaliim came.

13

The Nephaliim of Nu

The precious sons of Zion, comparable to fine gold,
How are they esteemed as earthen pitchers,
The work of the hands of the potter!
Even the sea monsters draw out the breast,
They give suck to their young ones:
The daughter of my people is become cruel.

—Lamentations 4:3

Art, like Nature, has her monsters,
Things of bestial shape and with hideous voices.

—Oscar Wilde

A GREAT NEPHAL CALLED Azarel-e-ath-Tigath-Ti-Gasamon, received word of a people living in the mountains above Shinar, towards Van. Azarel-Tigath-Gasamon set forth from the Vast Expanse and strode across the Great Plain, through the cities of men and nephaliim. Azarel journeyed many months towards the mountains in search of these people that were rumoured to exist. He desired them in his heart similar to the animals he sought out and consumed. He decimated the population of mountain ibex and ibenox, those stout-horned ox-sheep of the mountains, while he journeyed that way, and killed many small peoples and tribes that he came across. He reached the passes of the river Oryx that leads up to the mountains around the Valley of Nu above the plain of Shinar in the south. There the cherubim of Phirst slew him with the terrible fire swords. He was cut down and died. His body decayed and his great skeleton lay beached under the heavens for many years.

Word of his death reached the Fallen Ones whose anger seethed because one of their sons had fallen at the hand of God. They came up together against the cherubim of Phirst, but they had no light and could not press the cherubim who were too mighty for them. Instead they cursed the angels and their swords many months, uttering terrible oaths and speaking deep and evil spells against them. Then they went away full of wrath and decimated huge numbers of people to honour Azarel-Tigath-Gasamon their son. They forced men to heap up huge stones over the bones of their fallen son. Even today that mountain of stones can still be seen, for nothing will grow there. The earth was grieved because of the nephaliim and the soil was cursed.

Nu knew nothing of the coming of Azarel-Tigath-Gasamon. He heard only tales as animals and men came up his valley, fleeing the approach of that evil nephal and then from the Watchers when they came to confront the cherubim. Nu considered what he heard, but trusted Unos, and he and his family continued the work he had received in the vision.

After the death of Azarel-Tigath-Gasamon, stories passed up the valley, disturbing things, but the family of Nu gave them no weight. They continued to toil year after year, believing in Unos and the work they had been given to do. It was a great work, and it was their lives.

Huge herds of animals came through their region. As the herds passed small numbers of individual animals remained behind in the valley of Nu, which is in Van. These creatures survived among all the creatures that were utterly destroyed by the nephaliim and the perversion of the Fallen Ones, those Watchers of old. In this time the great paraceratheriums, those tall muscular tree-eating camel-horses passed in to oblivion, eaten and consumed by fire in massive pits. Their offspring were hunted and harpooned, roped and netted in the marshes; they were shot and killed by the machines and traps that the nephaliim and evil men made.

All the great flying beasts were also killed. Only the small ones remained: the eagles, and the hawks and the sea birds that were able to fly far out to sea and float on the waves, where the nephaliim did not come for the sea spoke to them of judgement. The nephaliim created great shooting machines that filled the skies with death and the great pterasaurs were all brought down, their majestic kites no longer worshipping God across the skies as they soared colorful and resplendent with outstretched wings.

During his time, Arook-Anuth-Amun-ni-Tagasar a great nephal of JNN climbed up into the mountain fastnesses below Kaz-Pian and plundered the rookeries and nests of the great pterosaurs. It was rare in his days to see a pterosaur gliding through the skies, for they feared the nephaliim and man on the plains below. When one was seen, it was immediately hunted down and taken, so evil were men. They conspired continually to have everything, yet received nothing. Their lives were vain and empty; they destroyed and killed all the beautiful things God had made, and cut down and destroyed the forests, and polluted the waters that made everything pleasant.

The nephaliim had large rupturing sores on their flesh from their evil blood and from fighting. Their stench acted as a warning to the animals that could sense their coming on the wind. Loathsome fluids flushed down their living corpses and they lived continually soiled. Using knowledgeable arts taught by their fathers, they devised methods to create disease that deformed animals and men so that they became greatly misshapen. This woe was added to creation on top of the corruption their fathers wrought within the blood of living things. The Watchers of Flesh and their nephaliim offspring toyed with creatures for they were fascinated yet jealous of the life within them. They experimented over many generations and destroyed many orders of animals with their perversions. Cross-species became weak and no longer produced any offspring. By this method many animals vanished from the earth and terrible strains of disease went out across the land infecting and maiming man and beast. This evil upon evil grieved God's heart as his eyes looked to and fro across the table of the earth for men who would turn to him and seek his help from the oppression of the nephaliim. But none were righteous; none remembered the Throne of Love, Unos or the holy things. Only Nu and his sons among all the men of that day made the annual offerings up to heaven. It was the only sweet fragrance of goodness that came up to God from the earth which was otherwise only despair and destruction. Man and beast were thwarted. But slowly the great ship in Van took shape.

Nu-Anna, the wife of Nu, was a great singer. She sang this song with her sons' wives around the fires of Nu,

In the days of dark
  When things were not
God came and breathed
  And heartily spoke.
Light was opened, the world began
  It was good and grand
For God breathed forth.
  He made a man, Oné,
Placed him in Phirst
  Made a woman from his side
Cleaved him there
  Safe to hide.
Then came a serpent
  Shining and vengeful
Deceiving he was
  Red evil devil.
Sa-Tan his name, drew them away
  Weeping in heaven, on earth, to this day.
Fled the children Oné and Eva
  Ever distant, broken a-sunder.
But Unos was wrathful
  Cursing that snake.
Punished he was, fire and lake.
  Turning to mankind, full of compassion
Plans he had laid, with Father the Faithful.
  Through many years, evil was brewing
Unos had light, pillars, and teaching.
  But man would not listen
In futility abandoned,
  Down through the eons, lost in great poison.
But came up a generation
  Of ancient wisdom,
En-Ocha, Methu-Saleh and my husband.
  For God had a plan
Of earth and redemption.
Unos is working his purposes out,
  as eons are passing;
LoGoi is working his purposes out,
  time is a-drawing -
Nearer and nearer cometh the plan-
When earth will be filled
  with the glory of God,
as the waters cover the sea.
  From eastern to western,

> where'er foot has trod,
> By the mouth of his messengers
> His voice will go out.
> Give ear to Me, ye continents—ye isles,
> Give ear to Nu-Anna.
> The earth will be filled with the glory of God,
> as the waters cover the sea.[1]

By the fiftieth year Nu and his family had completed the circumference of the great ship. Its upper ribs reached up to the heavens like beseeching hands crying out to God above. The lower deck was completed and became a great storage level for the fouling of the animals to be housed above. Nu and his sons sealed it all with pitch, a paste they made from bitumen and tar that welled up from cracks in the ground at the western end of their valley. At the end of the fiftieth year they progressed into the second tier, building up the great vessel from the ground, tier upon tier according to all the plans given to Nu.

The four wives of Nu, Jahf, Sem, and Hamaa alone supported their husbands and the building of the great ship. They gathered food and cared for the homes and clothed their husbands, because the men worked solely on the vessel.

Every seventh season Nu left the work and went out into the forests and valleys and talked to the peoples for sixty-six days, but none of them would listen or believe his religion. Instead they laughed at the story of his great ship. They ate, and drank and caroused and slept like the animals did, and all their waking days their simple hearts and minds thought only about their needs and their pleasures. They lived hidden from the terrors of the Great Plain, but still they never considered Unos or the ways of their ancestors Oné and Eva. But Nu went out to them every seventh season and talked for sixty-six days every seventh season, then he returned to the building of the ship.

When Nu talked to the peoples God watched over him. He often came to the passes of the mountains and looked down and saw the vast blackness spread out across the Great Plain. He could see in the distance erupting volcanoes, and he heard stories of the great nephals who oppressed men so mightily. Great God forbade Nu to go down to the Great Plain, even though he desired to go. In his heart Nu longed for the earth to return to goodness, and its decay and corruption played on his

---

1. With acknowledgment to Arthur Campbell Ainger, 1841–1919.

mind all his days. But God knew how very evil the earth had become and he would not allow Nu to go down. So Nu travelled the valleys and forests around Phirst where his ancestors had lived. In the forty-ninth year of the building of the ship, when Nu had travelled further than he had before looking for people to tell of the coming judgement and of Unos, he came to the shores of the Kaz-Pian. Nu saw great destruction and the ancient remains of war. Everywhere, all was ruined and bones lay bleached everywhere, decayed in the sun and wrapped in the sands. Decades before nephaliim had followed the rivers up to the coastlands of the sea from PaZuZu in the west and from JNN in the south. They built kingdoms around the circumference of Kaz-Pian and enslaved all the peoples of the region. But they were kept from coming up the valley of Nu in the west by the mists that God drew up from the Oryx. Nephaliim and the men of this region consumed all the creatures and trees of the valley and fought. The excess of the nephaliim overwhelmed the people. They departed that place and separated themselves from each other, prideful and arrogant, and went away to the northern and southern places to plunder and oppress others. For wherever nephaliim came, there was destruction, death and ruination of every kind. Nu picked through the plains and studied the ruin of everything and noticed how even the ground had grieved and been stricken and gone into lament and mourning. Nu was a man of the soil and understood the arts of the ground. He found there hideous ornaments of evil men, made from the bodies of their victims, drinking vessels and containers for water, and weapons fashioned from the bones of their foes, and all sorts of other evil things made from shrunken heads, teeth, bones and hair. He saw also the remains of the evil machines the nephaliim had made. Nu was grieved and he left that place and never returned, burning his shoes in a fire as he left that sad and evil valley.

As the generations passed, the nephaliim became more and more distorted. They grew in height but their forms mutated and they became hideous and perverted of flesh and were most fearsome and loathsome. In the days after Oné they had been in the appearance of large men, but now they became more like monsters as the mothers the Watchers took were ever less pure with the seed of Oné.

Within their bodies, the nephaliim gathered the seed of their fathers the Watchers, of man, and of the beasts of the land and the birds of the air. Some even began to crawl upon the earth because they could no longer walk upright for their limbs no longer supported them. Compared to men, they retained some of their radiance and their great height and strength, and this is why men worshipped them as gods. The Watchers spread amongst men hideous religions devised to feed their lusts and thus destroy them all. Men remained afraid of the power within the nephals. The nephals fed on the torment of men, on human despair, and fear, and hatred; they fed on any and all passions that man had, for the nephaliim were dead on the inside and yearned to feel human things. Nephaliim had neither the spirits of their fathers nor the souls of men inside them; rather, all that existed was a gnawing hunger that they could never satiate. They were the unlawful hybrid of rebellion and pollution; creatures that God never intended to inhabit the earth. This kernel of hell was their nature and it burned within them from the time they were made of women by their evil fathers.

Nu and his family studied all the animals that came into the valley and became greatly learned in the ways of all the creatures. His sons and their wives studied and cared for various creatures. They learned their ways and kept some of them penned on farms, fed, and tamed many. But those that were deformed and perverted from places where nephaliim had perverted flesh, Nu killed all these, for they were in pain and suffered life because of the seed within them. So, no animals of these polluted lines survived to pass on the seed of corruption in the valley of Nu.

Every seventh season, just before his great journeys to visit the people in the mountains and neighbouring forests, Unos came to Nu and encouraged him in dreams. He talked with him, and spoke to him of the great ship and how it would bless the whole earth. Nu was encouraged and strengthened in the labour that he and his sons did.

In the seventieth year, the family of Nu completed the second tier and closed in the great moulded planks that circled the vast craft. The wood was strong, moulded and fixed together with resins that set as hard as stone. While Jahf and Hamaa worked above, Sem covered the second tier with pitch inside and out, so that it set fast. The ship stood black against the green plain in the valley of Van where Nu and his family sheltered from the seas of evil and destruction that raged around them.

Also in this year, the nephaliim reached the most northern lands bordered by the great deep of the sea that circled the Great Plain. From here, accompanied by men, they set out along the coast and gradually moved west and east along it following the trails of the great herds of animals that had departed from men centuries before. Everywhere they went, all things were consumed, polluted and perverted and in despair. There was no peace; only wars, and fires and torments for both man and beast. God saw it all and knew that as long as he allowed men and nephals to continue in the earth nothing would be left. All would be consumed and from the dust and death the Watchers would come and dance upon the earth a hideous revelry against God amongst their evil children. So it would continue, rebellion upon rebellion, evil upon evil, darkness upon ever-deepening darkness, until men were lost to the light. Unos' eyes scanned the earth looking for any men whose hearts turned above and who cried for help, but none did. Only in the valley of Nu was there light among men.

The great enemy, Sa-Tan who dwelt in the center looked across all he had made. All men and the Watchers worshipped him through their vile religions and evil sciences. Sa-Tan had contempt for the earth and his soul burned hatefully against men. He desired to completely dispossess them of the earth so that only nephaliim remained. He rejoiced exultantly over everything the sons of the Fallen Ones had done.

Some of the great nephals were remembered in the legends of men after the Waters: such as Kronos, the Titans, and the sons of TiaMaT. In the Vast Expanse, on the peaks and high plateaus to the north, which later were islands, there was a fearsome warrior nephal of the Fallen One CHaRuN. He was called Heracleos, a fearsome creature. The beast went to and fro in that place and killed many men and attacked his brothers the nephaliim of that region. He boasted in his strength and went about the earth continually challenging all and attacking and defeating anything that withstood his pride. He was an arrogant creature and desired only to fight and conquer, boasting in his strength.

In and around the dominion of his father GoRgoNoS, Heracleos butchered the fierce saber-toothed cats and other predatory beasts in the hinterland and the nephaliim high places of Nemea and Argolis. He used clubs, nets, bows and arrows and armies of spearmen over many years to capture these bold creatures, and massacred them all. Heracleos joyed in taking these large beasts on hand-to-hand. A well-built and very strong nephaliim, he could even subdue the other nephals round about. Heracleos was able to vanquish mighty creatures by shooting them through with missiles before advancing with a large metal club he kept across his back, or tearing them to pieces with his bare hands.

After these contests terrible victory cries were heard, rolling across the hills like primal screams from the time of the great fall. Heracleos was forever boasting in his accomplishments and challenging all to be subdued. He skinned the spotted and tawny cats and used their pelts as his heraldry and attire. He enjoyed walking in boots made of toughed cat skins hardened in urine and blood, with their pelts over his shoulders, and wearing a loin cloth made of smilodon skin. He had men fashion the long sabre teeth of his prey in to ornaments and necklaces that he wore around his neck, adorning a mighty shield, and decorating the handle of his great club.

After all the cats were gone from GoRgoNos, Heracleos heard of a large serpent with many heads that lived in a swamp to the south. He traveled many days until at last he found the swamp that concealed a large remnant sauropod with a long neck and a massive serpentine tail. The creature hid itself in a vast swamp in AZaZeL. He tracked and cornered it in the swamp, but the serpent would not venture out. So, Heracelos drained the swamp with enslaved human labor and exposed many smaller sauropods, all of which were attacked. He hacked off their necks and tails which the creatures swung with ferocity at their assailants. But all the creatures were subdued, which lead to the legend of the many-headed serpent called the Hydra living in the swamps. When those creatures were all undone, Heracleos and his evil men burned all the creatures. He took the head of the great sauropod and buried it's skull beneath a large rock and piled up many other rocks over it as a high place to Heracelos and forced men to worship him there and exalt in him and his defeat of the great creatures.

After the demise of the sauropods in the swamp of AZaZeL, and the departure of nephaliim from that place, men came and hunted the fresh water crabs that abounded in the waters, until they were all netted, speared and eaten. In this way the swamps were stripped of all the living creatures in them and around them. Eventually the waters eked away due to the diversions and re-channeling used to drain the land, and it became dry and desolate where once it had been lush and abounding with the life God had made there. And only the wind was heard in that place.

After these years, and ever restless, Heracelos moved eastward with his army and attacked the men and nephals of INCuBu. In this land between respites in the many battles he agitated, Heracleos hunted and killed the large wild quadrupeds, boars and other mammals of the deep forests. On the plains were also many men and many horses, striped, mottled and of different species and colors. These also Heracleos and his retinue attacked and subdued. Not all the horses were consumed, for they spread out across the land and avoided men and nephals in massive herds with the other herding creatures of those days. Heracleos drove the herds with fire, used them to trample men and their chiefs and devastate their villages and towns.

Also in the south, in TiaMaT towards the sea where the Ankylosoi dwelled, was a mountainous region. In these rocky parts lived herds of giant auroch. Men feared their ferocity, but Heracleos took to them and over many decades subdued and destroyed all the mighty auroch of that place. He built temples with their bloodied skulls and horns, which he prized as trophies. The larger auroch bulls Heracelos hunted and shot through with missiles and attacked them with spears and swords and his mighty club.

Around the lakes in the Great Plain that fed off some of the high places Heracelos and his army killed many of the large flying birds. They lit fires on the ridges and high places. As the birds wheeled into the air, they made great sport of bringing them down with various contrivances. This was a favorite pastime of this nephal when he was not engaged in some campaign or subduing peoples or testing himself against beasts of the land.

Towards the end of his health Heracleos went beyond the Great Plain and out into the southern Vast Expanse, where no men ventured. Traveling alone, he was poisoned by the vents and gases that came up in those places and was greatly weakened. Returning to the Great Plain he was attacked by packs of large dogs from Geryon and was also set upon by large companies of men. But he bribed them with the offer of herds of wild cattle. These he drove into their villages where he settled for a time only to betray the men later, when he was recovered, burning their villages with fire and massacring them in the confusion. Heracleos trapped and killed the dogs that had hounded him with traps and pits and poisoned arrows. Eventually he tired of that place and moved back north.

After hundreds of years his teeth became broken and worn away so Heracleos fed on fruits and crops and no longer ate the tough meats he had feasted on all his life. Two kings of men and their armies called the Hadoi and the Cerberoi came together under their nephaliim and pushed Heracelos and his slave armies back towards the north, where the great nephal began to fade. He crawled away to the rocky tops in ZeMu and there, away from the eyes of the living crawled away into a crack beneath the roots of the land and slithered his heaping bulk into deep holes. There he lay, drinking and hungering. He became a worgm, lost to life except in the legends of his conquests that spanned the dominions of GoRgoNoS, AZaZeL, INCuBu TiaMaT and the Vast Expanse. He was the first nephaliim to venture that far south into ZeMu. He was one of the greatest of the nephaliim.

Even so, the Waters undid him when they came and drowned him in his filth and with mud from the earth in his darkened crack beneath the mountains of ZeMu.

Heracelos is remembered to this day in the legends of the people of that place but they remembered only his pride, and his deeds, not the evil of the creature, for he was only half a man and had no soul.

Many seasons after the demise of Azarel-Tigath-Gasamon who was killed by the guardian cherubim, a brother nephal called Ma-Goth came into the land and heard the tales of how Azarel-Tigath-Gasamon had been slain. He thought long about the stories and they intrigued him. So, he sent spies to the lands around that place, near to old Phirst, and in time learned the parameters of Phirst guarded by the cherubim. He also learned of the valleys near Van where Nu and his family and the peoples of the forests lived. Ma-Goth believed that his brother nephal had gone there and discovered some great secret and for this had been slain. So, Ma-Goth stole up into the mountains and circled around the high places around Phirst and studied that land for many months. He watched and waited. Ma-Goth actually came to the pass that looked down into the valley in which Nu constructed the great ship. He wondered at the thing, and bent his will to its destruction and to smashing and burning its form, for he feared it. Nephals despised anything that was not of themselves, so arrogant and self absorbed were they.

But his hunger betrayed him. So burning was the emptiness within him that he raged through the forests and hunted and consumed many of the men who lived there. Nu heard of it and set out to see and confront the great nephal. But Nu never found Ma-Goth, for God sent warrior teraphim and they guided Ma-Goth by intriguing lights at night and caused him to fall into a deep cavern. His mighty bones cracked at the bottom of the chasm and broke. Ma-Goth bellowed with rage and cursed the lights that had led him. People found him broken at the bottom of the cavern. They had suffered terribly at the hand of the nephals in the outlaying areas, so they cut brush and foliage and tossed it down from far above until it covered him. Then they threw down torches and the brush caught and burned Ma-Goth as he lay broken. His great misshapen hulk was burned alive with fire and he raged and screamed like a giant beast, for he could not get out, and was burned. After many days, the people crept down by ropes and pulleys. They found the cooled and charred remains and ate Ma-Goth and picked his bones clean so the powerful seed of Ma-Goth might go into the tribe.

The people grew haughty after killing a god, a mighty nephal. Having taken him into themselves they grew arrogant towards Nu. Ma-Goth's blood poisoned their minds and they began to conspire that perhaps they could also kill and consume the god Nu. But God kept them away.

Years later a third nephal of PaZuZu came toward Van from the north. This creature came down across the mountains and into the forest of Van unawares of Nu and the great ship. He was met by another nephal, a hideous and misshapen beast that Unos inspired to come across the mountain range from the east and the kingdoms of Kaz-Pian. And these two became aware of each other by their great cries in the night from the hungers they suffered. The two sought each other out and attacked and fought each other. The one, called by men Rathma-Rama-Zod-Akon, vanquished his brother from the north and ate and consumed him. Akon then moved off to the north and the forests of Van and the valley of Nu were spared any more intrusions by nephaliim.

The Watchers of Flesh who had received the remnant light of the Watchers, continued to take to themselves daughters of men. They grew and brought forth nephaliim. But as the generations passed, their light began to fade and they brought forth less offspring. Women began to fail repeatedly in their bringing forth of the god men. Nephaliim could not bring forth children of their own making, so they enslaved men and animals having only contempt and hatred for them all. There was never a caring sentiment within the breast of a nephal towards man or beast. They kept such as alive as were of use to them in their schemes and conspiracies against each other, as did the mighty men. From the very beginning the Watchers hated and feared women the most, jealous of their power. So, they took them, and used them to procreate a race of beings upon the earth after their own kind. They feared greatly the Great

Man a woman was destined to bring forth against them, a redeemer of things. So they sought to destroy all of humanity and replace it with their own sons to stop the coming of the Great Man.

When not killed in war, or by murder, the nephaliim lived many years, longer than men, for they had eternal seed in their blood from their fathers the Watchers. They grew weak as they aged. And as they did so, to avoid being eaten and slaughtered by their stronger brothers, they crawled away into mountain fastnesses and down inside caves and into the roots of mountains where they hid themselves and hungered away in darkness and ruin.

> Near the foundation stones of the world
> Where evil powers lurk that are so old
> Even Sauron knows them not.[2]

They drank from the drippings of waters in the mountain deeps and from stagnant lakes, and there they lay, undying, and hungering in the darkness hidden from the fires and machines and teeth of their brothers. They grew weak and shrunken and became great worgms in the mountain roots, their limbs and arms withered away so that only their great loathsome bodies remained as sacks, drinking up the waters to assuage their unending thirst. They ate no more, and nothing could assuage their hunger within. Their hearts and minds were blackened with madness as they meditated all the evils they had done and could do, and every evil imagination they could conjure in the darkness blackened their minds. They were impotent and could do nothing in their flesh. Such ones became the lost nephaliim of the earth and they too were all destroyed when the waters of God came. Though lost to the knowledge of men, God saw where each one lay and saw the overwhelming of each one as it gasped out its life in deep cracks and holes under the mountains. They were crushed and drowned by blackened waters and filth in their stone tombs lost to the light of day. Their bones will be found in ages afterward by the men of later times. They were indeed the sons of darkness and unworthy of the earth. God bound them to the earth. They were undone by the waters that had sustained them in their holes of despair. In this way, the earth had its justice against the nephaliim by undoing them in rock with waters that crushed and drowned them. And the great worgms perished.

2. J. R. R. Tolkien, *Lord of the Rings*.

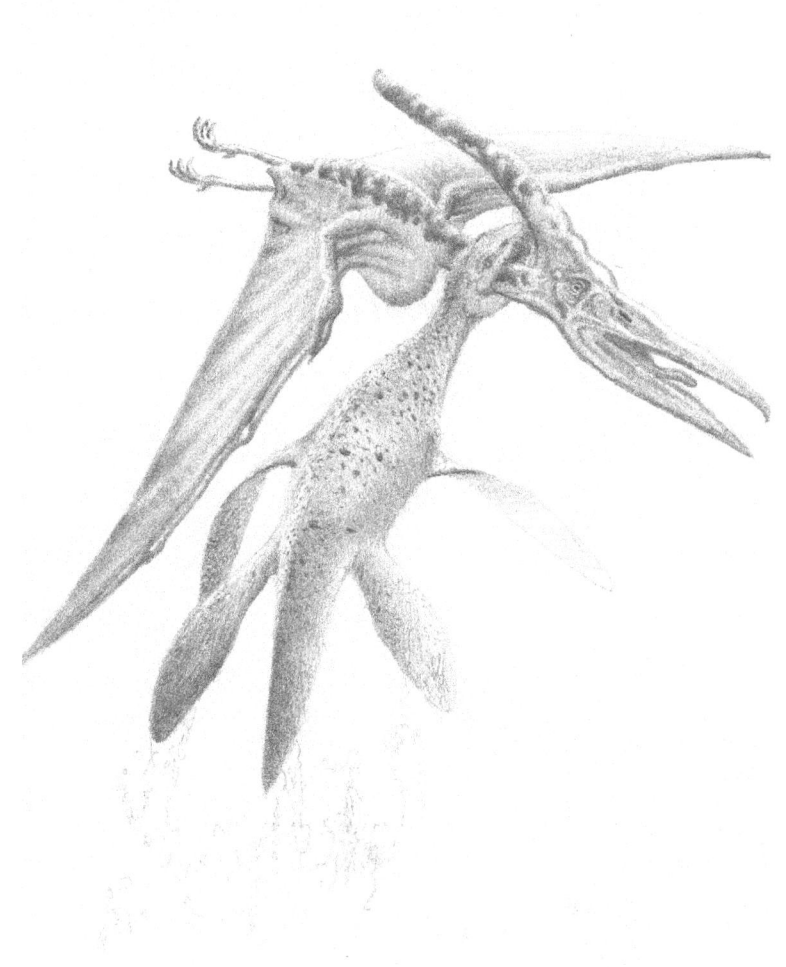

A marine crypto-clidfoi grabbing a flying pteradon

14

Men come against the Great Ship

Great words of prideful men are ever punished
With great blows; and in old age,
Teach the chastened to be wise.

—Sophocles, *Antigone*

Ignorance breeds monsters
To fill up the vacancies of the soul
That are unoccupied by the verities of knowledge.

—Horace Mann

WHILE THE BUILDING OF the great ship progressed, the family of Nu built their lives around understanding and caring for animals of various kinds.

Jahf husbanded herds of cera-tops. He particularly loved the colorful hooded proto-ceratopsians. He cared for the crested oviraptors that were swift of foot. These creatures flashed brilliant luminescent colors from their crests and sang lyrical songs.

Hamaa loved the mottled and aspen-colored three-toed horses: meso-hippus, para-hippus, proto-and dino-hippus. He also had many equus. The huge but gentle blue and red para-ceratherms as well as bron-tops were herded among the colored horses. Hamaa's creatures included the woolly mammoth and elephant and two great mammuts and mastodon. He also had four brightley-colored stegosaur that were rare in those days. These, along with giraffe, camels and rhinoceros came with him into the ship. Hamaa was the most skilled animal husband beside Nu. He learned many things from his father concerning the ways of the creatures of the earth, how to husband them and control them with skill and knowledge that men will not understand in later days.

Sem loved the swift, feathered velociraptors that herded with theropoda, mononykus, coelophysis and tenontosaurs. He had some moschops and twelve great platybelodons that grazed in the marshes around the ship. These were very colorful with unique feathers that could change their colors into luminescent hues. In the trees, Sem nurtured many species of notharctus and various kinds of arch-aeopteryx. These animals were tuneful and noisy, producing great shrills and cackles that continually filled the forests so that the trees rang with a cacophony of song.

All these animals fed from the rich abundance of vegetation that prospered all around the ship. They used their sharp and grinding teeth to strip and crush the plants for food. The more they pruned and stripped the trees and bushes, the more the vegetation responded and grew back. The stripping and weeding of growth caused the plant life to flourish even more. In areas where the animals did not feed, the plants did not flourish and prosper, and instead grew more slowly or became dormant.

Among all these creatures, the family of Nu fostered many other animals of their own liking besides the Nu-mastafoi.

In those days all the great pro-sauropods were extinguished so that there were none to come later with Nu into the ship. They were netted, trapped and destroyed by men and nephaliim, who hated them above all creatures because of their magnificence and grandeur. The nephals were jealous of their regal standing before the LoGoi. Since they were the greatest of God's creation, Sa-Tan despised them all the more. Great apatasaurs and plateosaurs, and diplodocus were trapped and bound in pits with great metal bindings. These beautiful creatures were tormented by the nephaliim when they were brought down so that they bellowed and groaned. Day after day, the cries from their mighty frames and their prolonged suffering went up to God, and it grieved him greatly. So malicious had men become under the oppression of the nephals, that they did not even allow these majestic beasts to die when they were caught, but kept them alive impaled within pits and bound with cruel entrapments designed to torment. Many were used as living food, meat carved from their bodies as they lived and suffered. These giants were tormented with lit fires and great serrated saws and hooks and spears until they bled to death or died of shock, starvation and dehydration. God despaired of ever creating these mighty creatures as he watched men and the vile nephaliim pollute his work and destroy them all with malice.

Away in the east in the eighty-first year of the building of the ship, a great she-leviathan, the mightiest and most majestic of all God's marine creatures, became beached within shallow waters off a peninsula. She was called Aoo-umm-aazzaootha for that was the sound of the great songs she made in the deep, calling to the great whales that she hunted. She sounded for the great shoals of eurhino-delphoi and pods of blue stenopterygius whom the Zamzummin of the coastlands called the Leaping Fish. Driven by Aoo's great echoing, the Leaping Fish often came close to shore. Their sport and play amazed men. They were caught with nets and harpoons, for their sweet flesh was greatly prized. The nephaliim pressed men out into boats to capture and net them, but the nephals would never go out into the oceans.

Although the nephaliim greatly feared the water, nevertheless they came to see the great creature. Using machines and weapons to rain down bolts and fire spears from the cliffs above, the monsters killed the massive creature. Men swam and sailed out to it and carved it up with cleavers and saws and took away the flesh. The nephaliim rejoiced over the demise of this queen of the earth. Until the Waters came, the sea where she beached was known as Ashak-Leviathan-Un-Zamzummin-Osh-Akalok-Nephaliim, which means in the ancient tongue, "Place where the Great One was Humbled by Osh the Nephal." Osh had his men pull out the dead creature's massive teeth from its fearsome mouth. He shaped these in to a great helmet and a breastplate to wear. He even contrived to sew its skin to his skin to make himself more fearsome. Men worshipped him as a god, because of the great teeth and the skin. One of the great teeth bent forward over the crown of his head and was wrapped around the side of his face. When Osh was killed in centuries later in the wars of the PaZuZu and JNN nephals Amoth-Uma-Enom and Amoth-Agga-Og, the leviathan teeth were awed and greatly prized. Nephaliim battles were fought over them, and many perished trying to win them, for they were prized as talismans of strength and power. And so the teeth of that majestic beached leviathan avenged her, for they caused the demise of many nephals desiring to posses them.

In those days of Aoo, some of the coastal-dwelling men escaped from the nephaliim kingdoms by boats and went away to islands south of the Ankylosoi and the nepahls of PaZuZu. These were the islands and seas where the peradons flew. The men fought and warred with each other. The island sanctuaries became traps into which they stumbled for they destroyed each other in their lust to control the food sources of the islands. None of those men who escaped to the islands, or their offspring, survived, for they all fell by killing and eating each other until the islands were as treacherous as the mainland. Over time all the plants for food and the island trees were destroyed so no boats could be made; there was no getting away and so they all perished on the islands to which they had fled.

After the demise of the pro-sauropods, the great winged pterodactyls and pteradons lived on, protected for many years by the great oceans. Their mighty wings carried them over the waters, hovering over the seas like great bats in the fruiting forests, harvesting fish with their pulsing luminescence that drew great fishes up from the deep. The mighty pteradons would scoop up in their powerful toothless bills the hard-shelled dunkleosteus and the blue/red axel-rod-ichthys. The agile and rapid swimming crypto-clidfoi would rocket upwards behind streaming ribbons of phosphorescence shimmering up from the deep and snatch the hovering pteradons, before plunging back into the foaming ocean. They would tear them apart, swallowing whole chunks of flesh in the reddening sea. Pterotacyls and pteradons survived on separated islands to which they flew to roost and breed. However, on the mainland coasts of the Great Plain, the nephaliim came and killed them all and consumed every egg they could find. What the nephaliim left behind, men came and raided so that the mighty kites no longer roosted and bred there. Their numbers diminished. Nephaliim used shooting machines to hunt the great sky creatures until they were all but gone. The tiny rham-pho-hycoi survived in the forests and coastlands of the Vast Expanse, and Nu took them into his ship as well as a pair of pteradons and two petradactyl whom God brought to him in the valley of Van on easterly breezes.

Great pestilences racked the earth because of the intense warfare and death. Disease percolated and grew in the cities of decaying corpses that littered the landscape. Hundreds of thousands of men perished with terrible wasting plagues. So virulent did some of these diseases become, even some of the nephaliim succumbed. Men suffered terribly but the nephaliim knew which plants and roots to ingest to preserve their bodies, for they had this knowledge from their fathers. Although they were more intelligent than men, having the seed of their fathers within, which came from heaven, this seed only caused them to do more evil.

During this time, men died and wasted away from parasites and worms and internal eruptions that poured fluids forth and poisoned their blood. Their skins blackened and ruptured, they suffered from rashes and boils; their limbs rotted so that they could not walk or use their arms and hands. Men perished in untold misery, in lonely pain and despair as pestilence swept across the earth in those times. None of these things came near the valleys of Van, for Nu and his family were faithful to Unos who preserved them with mists and winds that shielded them from these evil things.

Once the circumference of the great ship was completed to the floor of the second level, the families moved into the construction. The wives of Nu nurtured small furry creatures within the ship and several striped and mottled cats were kept as well as shrews, rodents of many types and colors, small birds and raptors.

Hamaa-Oz-Olloc kept several brilliantly colored sailed dimetrodons and pely-cosaurs that angled their great sails at each other in display and alarm. Their sails were very colorful from the fruits they ate, and delighted the women. The creatures changed color according to mood so that Hamaa and the women knew when any were sick or about to give birth. The women made large sailed hats and headpieces from woven flaxes and feathers that they dyed and painted like the sails of the pely-cosaurs and dimetrodons. This became a fashion among the women of Nu's family, who made for themselves colorful woven materials that they shaped up in to magnificent headwear to resemble these delightful animals.

Because the men worked hard on the ship, they did not concern themselves with such things, except for Jahf who was tattooed on his forehead and lower harms like his mother Nu-Anna after the custom of her clan. The men wore tanned skins about their bodies and had no need for upper wear, which left them free to hammer and saw as they built the great ship.

Jahf-Anna became wise in the making of colors. She discovered ways of blending soils and barks, roots and leaves with the juice of fruits from which she made exotic fine-smelling pastes and colors that will be unknown to future men. Some of these the women used as adornments and others were boiled and distilled to make paints, which the women used to color and enrich all the things they used. At the time of the sacred gift offerings, when the fires of God came, the family of Nu painted themselves in honor of Unos using the skill of Jahf-Anna.

With the help of her daughters, Nu-Anna made for Nu a great cloak, which he wore on his travels to the peoples. It was light and hung just above his ankles. It was softly lined and had openings so Nu could cool himself. It was decorated with bright feathers and oviraptor crests, which were cut and stitched in attractive designs all over the cloak. It was a thing of exceeding beauty such as other men did not make elsewhere. Other men never had sufficient peace to contemplate the manufacture of such things. Such knowledge came only from the tranquillity around the great ship and was nurtured only in the family of Nu where there was peace.

The women furnished the homes of the families within the great ship with every beautiful and comfortable textile and covering. There were pillows and felts and carpets and coverings made of all manner of materials. This made the ship a pleasant and comfortable place for the family of Nu.

With the help of Nu's skill in metallurgy, Nu-Anna and Sem-Anna-Hill-Ashak created wondrous jewellery of gold, amethyst, silver and sparkling alloys from the metals of the earth. They used all manner of minerals, such as will be lost in the future, to devise wondrous works of jewellery. The four wives cast these metals into creative fancies that were used to adorn the living quarters inside the grounded ship as it grew. Some of these wondrous objects remained as heirlooms in the great households after the Waters but were lost in the wars and confusions that will reign after Ba-Bel is abandoned.

Sem made furniture and installations for the interior, for he was skilled in intricate arts. He worshipped God with his skill and God took pleasure in all that Sem worked in this way.

In the eighty-third year the evil peoples came again to the ship, but this time with a mighty man called Ox-Muta as their chieftain. He was very tall and well built, a powerful and dominating man. He had great horns lashed to a circlet around his face so that he looked most fearsome, like the yawning mouth of some savage beast. He persuaded the people that the great ship was evil. They drove the Nu-mastafoi back, and heaped up cut brush and woods around the ship as they had thrown down upon Azaeal. In that year they tried to burn the ship of Nu. But so hard was it and so weathered by eight decades of building, no fire would take to it, and the people gave up and went away.

They camped now in the valley around the ship and made their homes in the valley and forests. Nu and his sons brought all the animals from their outlaying farms and wild pastures into the ship so that they were safe. The animals went in and out from the ship and grazed around it.

The people of the valley were evil. They derided Nu and became emboldened and mocked him. Nu and his ship became an object of derision so that whenever a man passed solids from his body, he would scratch a sign of the ship in the sand before he defecated on it. The great ship became known as a fouled thing and Nu the god of fouling. Such was the foolishness of men and their evil and empty thoughts.

God grieved deeply for the orders of all the animals that were extinguished. He ached because of all the pain man and beast endured continually because of the seed of the Fallen Ones within them. He hated the great slaughter that all suffered. God grieved that man was so corrupted and oppressed, but he had no grief for the nephaliim, for they were an abomination to him. They were black inside; they had no mercy, no love, and no forethought for anything good, just contempt and hatred continually. God's wrath burned against the Fallen Ones and the nephaliim offspring of the Watchers because of the corruption that came upon the earth after he had made it so wondrous. For this was their worship, to defile everything God had made before his sight. There was no turning them, for they had no soul, and were ever evil, untrustworthy, deceitful and conniving. They plotted murders and death and torment from morning till night.

But Nu went out to the men in the valley and talked to them about the great ship and of Unos. None of the people considered Nu's words. They were like dumb beasts on the plain.

The great ship grew like a fortress. It had a mighty fence of palisades around it because of the emboldened people coming up the valley and approaching the ship, something they had not done before. Inside the fence Nu and his family were safe. At this time God caused waters to come up from under the ground in the upper valley as a sign and to protect Nu and his family from Ox-Muta. The water flowed down the valley to where the ship was being built. The water flooded the plain and came right up to the ship, so that it sat in a small shallow lake. Marshes grew around it, so that people could no longer live there and they departed. The waters surrounded Nu and his family and all their animals and they had peace from the neighbouring peoples. The sons of Nu built bridges and board walks across the marshes, so they could go to and fro into the nearby forests and vales. On islands amid the marshes were pastures bordered by lush vegetation. Here Nu and Sem gathered many animals and housed them in corrals and farms connected with pathways and bridges to the ship that sat at the center in its shallow lake of water.

In the one-hundred-and-eighteenth year from the beginning of the construction of the ship, Nu's grandfather Methu-Saleh grew weak and men talked of it. His name was a sign and meant, "while I live, the waters shall not come." God also caused many new animals to appear in the valley. They came in small numbers, eluding men and the nephaliim. They came seeking Nu by an instinct of God. They sensed a great foreboding and were drawn to the valley of Nu. This same instinct remains in creatures before great quakes and eruptions occur in the skins of the earth. It is why animals migrate in large numbers to avoid the cold and the changing of the seasons. But in those days there were no seasons and no weather because the great canopy above the land was still intact except for the great tear through which came the flaming mountain of the Watchers and through which men could glimpse the vanquished teraphim glittering out in the heavens–the lost of the East Gate.

Jahf and Hamaa completed the great roof of the ark. The great hull rose up and curved inward toward the top. They lined this across with massive structural beams and latticed it with interweaving widths of wood that bound it strongly together. Down the central seam they built a trench and walled it around to a height of three feet. They housed the trench over with a smaller sloping roof and in the raised sides they left narrow slits through which air ventilated the ship. This was the uppermost story, where Nu and his family lived and where they could view the sky, and receive the light, and see all the animals beneath them. The structure of the great ship represented the order of things. Before the Fallen Ones usurped the sovereignty of man, God had set humanity above the animal kingdoms. Man was at the top of the great ship, with all the animals beneath him ranked according to their orders.

Nu's family lined the walls and roof with thick layers of pitch that hardened and shrank. This drew every fibre of the construction tight within itself. On the outside of the boat they did not paint any thing, for

God instructed Nu to leave the exterior completely untouched; black and with no adornment. Inside the ship there were wondrous workings and skilled woodwork and woven tapestries and creative things of great beauty.

In the one-hundred-and-nineteenth year of the ship building–that is Nu's seventeenth seventh-season, the last year he went out to the people for sixty-six days–Nu went out much further and talked with any manner of man he could find. The people he found stood far off and laughed at Nu and mocked him. None believed what he said. Men cursed him and his great ship. They called, saying Unos was dead. Others shouted that when Methu-Saleh died they would take his body and burn it with fire and consume it among all the tribes and gather his greatness into them. But they feared Nu and no one ever laid a hand on him or threw any object or raised any weapon against him. Inside they feared his strength and also the great dogs that accompanied him and seemed under his power. Nu returned at the end of the one-hundred-and-nineteenth year after great wanderings. He was greatly discouraged by the folly and evil of men that went on everywhere. He grieved for justice in the earth among the downtrodden of men and he wept bitterly night after night for all the evil things that he had seen. Nu-Anna comforted him.

Out in the world the nephaliim grew more evil. Their vice and the oppression of the human race knew no restraint. The onslaught was so great that men no longer lay with women and children were lost to the world, so that none perished in the Water that came. People were numb with toil and torment.

Sa-Tan and the Watchers motivated a great extermination of men, sensing a great foreboding. In that one-hundred-and-nineteenth year more men died at the hands of other men than in the entire seventh-season prior.

And then Methu-Saleh died.

15

Tears from Heaven

*The curse departs not
But falls upon all of the blood
Like the restless surge of the sea.*

—Sophocles *Antigone*

*O Lord, methought what pain it was to drown!
What dreadful noise of waters in my ears!
What sights of ugly death within my eyes!
. . . A thousand men that fishes gnaw'd upon
All scattered in the bottom of the sea.*

—William Shakespeare, *Richard III*

*I heard the sound of a thunder, it roared out a warnin'
Heard the roar of a wave that could drown the whole world
. . . It's a hard rain's a-gonna fall.*

—Bob Dylan, *It's a Hard Rain's A-Gonna Fall*

An angel came to Nu and told him to gather all the animals together that God had sent; certain numbers of various kinds. He was told to house them in the ship permanently. Nu was further instructed to fill the storehouses of the ship and to complete the great door and store up water in great pithoi sunk in large wooden sidings that circumvented each of the levels. Within seven months this was completed. The angel returned and told Nu that he and his family must go inside the ship. They closed the great door behind them and the angel sealed it with a fire that came from above so that no man could open or close the great door from within or without. It was sealed. There was no crack between the door and the side of the ship, for God sealed the wood together with a heavenly light that fused the timbers as one.

Seven days passed and nothing happened. Inside the ship, Nu, his family and all the animals were safe and waiting on God.

Outside, the waters of the valley all drained down into the earth, and the plain became dry and it made the people wonder. Ox-Muta, the mighty man with the great tusks came up with an army and there was fighting. Warriors came and looked at the ship that was an affront to them. They shook their fists at it and mocked the great edifice they could not conquer. When they could not find Nu, they came around the great ship and, calling for him, beat on the great hull with sticks and drums. Nu heard their voices. They laughed and told him they would burn his ship. They cut wood as they had done before and heaped it up against the great sides. They laughed and sang and danced in to the night yelling that they would burn the fortress of Nu with him inside, for Nu and the ship were an offence to them.

But the ship would not burn. Ox-Muta seethed against Nu, so he had a weapon made up against the side of the ship. It was a massive tree trunk slung on a structure built on skids. The head was bound with metal and crudely shaped. He called it "The Ox-Hammer." His men hauled it up against the ship, and beasts were engineered to haul it out on a sling away from the ship. It was then released and swung against the side of the vessel with a mighty boom. The sound startled the animals and the families within, but Nu trusted God. Day after day for seven days the Ox-Hammer crashed against the side of the ship. But an angel sat upon the tree and drew away the violence of the weapon so that no harm came to the wooden integrity of the ship. This angered Ox-Anna greatly. He and his men built pits of fire around the circumference of the ship. The people fed them day and night and continuously revelled around them. Although the ship was wreathed in flame and fire licked up the side and above into the sky, the flames never bit into the sidings of Nu's great ship.

At dawn on the seventh day, as Ox-Muta's men worked around the ship cursing and taunting at Nu inside and the mighty Ox-Hammer struck at the hull without rest, six large drops of water the size of a man fell, one after the other, from the sky and splattered on the sand in front of the sealed door. The men looked at this in wonder for they had never seen water fall from the sky. They prodded and poked the wet splotches on the sand and looked up at the sky. Ox-Anna was called. He took the mud in his hands and brushed the mud from heaven on himself and his private parts all the while cursing the Holy Ones above.

After the end of the first hour of that seventh day, a great rumbling was heard deep within the earth. The earth shook such as it never had before nor ever will again until the Time of the End. A crack opened down the seam of the Great Fissure. Massive waters came up from the deep and exploded under tremendous pressure within the ground shooting hundreds of miles up into the air. The noise was deafening and perforated the ears of men so that blood flowed down the sides of their heads. In confusion and utter chaos, they stumbled and crashed chaotically about, falling over each other as they watched the huge wall of water gushing up into the sky across a seam hundreds of miles wide. Such a noise had never been heard on the earth to that day. The water was a violent and massive torrent. As the massive geysers reached their climax, they stalled high in the air, held a moment, and then crashed down upon the earth. As the massive vertical tsunami came raining back down, the great windows of the firmament opened as well. Water from the heavens joined with the water of the earth as one, and poured down a violent rainstorm. The rain was savage and crushing. The water dashed men to pieces and everywhere animals and men were crushed down to the ground by the ruinous torrent that was like a huge hammer crashing onto the anvil of humanity.

As the deep was stirred, more geysers perforated the ground rending the skin of the earth. The oceans boiled and were thrusting up and great waves drew up and broke over the surface of the earth across Aoo-Umm, Ashak and in the north beyond the Vast Expanse. Everywhere titanic tsunamis rolled unrestrained across the flat earth sweeping clean everything across the face of the ground. The waves swept everything away, every creature, every tree, and every green thing. The soil was lifted, the land was scoured clean. Even the rocks were scrubbed free and swept away in great soups of destructive carnage and death. The embrace of the waters was total and nothing escaped the violent onslaught, so overwhelming and devastating was its awesome power.

God had given man one-hundred-and-twenty years to turn away from his evil, but no one turned.

People everywhere cried out. They ran and were crushed and tossed away by the unrelenting violence like dry husks in a storm. What voices were heard amid the screams were of cursing and savage anger, yelling against God and the water everywhere. Men's limbs flailed as they were tossed and carried away like tiny particles in an erupting volcano's spewing stack.

In the third hour, the great bridge of Gib-Ral-Tar at the farthest end of the Great Plain broke and the sea poured over hurling a cataclysmic surge down through the Great Plain past ZeMu and GoRgoNos. Hundreds of feet tall, it pulverised the kingdoms and cities, burning pits, industry, armies and machines of the nephaliim and men of the Great Plain, smashing the broken filth of millions of lives. It hurled against the rocks of the far eastern hills of ABRaXaS where the seat of Sa-Tan was, before rolling back on itself and crushing and smashing everything within its belly in a cauldron of swirling fury. Great overflowing torrents rushed across ABRaXaS and into the Great Fissure from the north. They were met by boiling ocean waves that had already inundated from the east. Together the ocean waters were picked up and hurled into the atmosphere by the spewing geysers from beneath along the now expanding fissure between PaZuZu and JNN, ripping open along the seam around the circumference of the earth.

Towards the end of the third hour, a great seam opened along the entire canopy above the earth. The pressure rent it apart along the yawning tear through which the Watchers had come and all the water of the firmament fell until the entire firmament collapsed and fell down. The few breathing things that were still alive saw this great and terrible collapse and–already driven mad by the noise and fury of the earth and sky convulsing around them– were smashed down from the mountain tops, passes, crags and hollows into which they had crept. They were washed out of every hole and ledge like dust before a mighty wind.

Into the fourth hour, amid the incredible force and violence, the water kept falling as showers of continuous weighty rain beat down until everything was drowned and buried beneath cleansing water.

Words cannot describe the horror and fierceness of the event, for God finally acquiesced and gave the earth freedom to release herself from vanity. Her wrath came like a fury against all the evils perpetrated on her as she acted to cleanse herself of the stain of man and the nephaliim and the Watchers from above. She showed no mercy.

Everywhere the nephaliim bellowed as they tried to shield themselves against the falling torrents. They thrust up against the rain with their shoulders and backs. Pushing their ugly heads up they tried to scream and curse God and the earth, but water filled their mouths and silenced their insults. They were horrified and overcome by the violence of the water from below and across the lands and from above. Nothing could withstand the fury of the earth as God released her. Countless herds of creatures perished and men everywhere were consumed. Nephaliim across the world were swept violently away and all the fires of the earth were quenched. Great plumes of hissing steam, smoke and dust went up into the place where the canopy had been dissolved away as the waters fell to the earth. The earth breathed out this dark smoke into the sky so that light was hidden as she exhaled all the evil that had been endured. The outer sky opened and great lightning and crashing thunder ravaged the atmosphere.

All things were undone. Stone and rock were ground and upheaved. So terrible and cataclysmic was this great judgement of water that everything was altered forever. The arrogance and haughtiness of men and the plague that was the nephaliim, and the all the work of the Fallen Ones against God, was crushed and swept away in those hours.

But north of Phirst God remembered Nu and the waters were restrained within his mountain valley. Water came from under the ground and lifted the great ship up into the sky and carried it off. It circled round in a great eddy between all the violent waves, storms and tumults that God allowed free upon the earth.

Within the ship, Nu and his family saw none of the destruction. They did not see the terrifying geysers, or the lightning, or heard the deafening tumults. Such violence would have driven them mad, so God caused all the animals and men within the ship to fall into a deep sleep. He cocooned them from the coming of the judgement. Towards the end of the sixth hour, when they awoke, they were aware the ship was lifted up and that they were moving. The great vessel swayed from side to side in the angry waves that now carried them aloft. It was completely dark, for the angel had forbidden Nu and his family to open any of the upper windows or to light any lamps. Neither could they go anywhere near to the upper decks, but were instructed to stay below wrapped within their furs and with all the animals and to wait the second day. And so they slept.

Outside everything was destroyed. The earth was scoured down to the bedrock and scrubbed completely clean.

Beneath the mountainous waves and the water now filling the earth from above, even the crust of the ground itself began to break up and was rent by quakes. The land was moved under the enormous weight and violence of the water. Great pieces sank and other pieces rose up and massive cracks opened in the seam of the earth and swallowed whole land shelves. Jagged ridges of rock were thrusting up. Between the expanding seams huge continental plates slid and shifted on the liquid magma boiling beneath. Everywhere huge clouds of mixed vapours fled into the sky above and wrapped the atmosphere in a cloudy shroud. Pangea, Gondwana and Lurasia, that trinity of great continents God made at first, broke into pieces. There was indescribable violence deep in the earth such as man cannot imagine. The land itself convulsed and broke under the pressure of the massive waters pressing down from above. Rock turned in to liquid and then into gas and rotated around the globe. The earth itself tilted on its axis and began to wobble. The magnetic axis shifted. This was the earth vomiting all the filth of its travail out of itself so that it might be cleansed of the poison that had come down to it. God allowed the earth twelve months–one for each of the fallen Watchers–for the waters to cleanse the ground.

The Fallen Ones and Sa-Tan were utterly terror struck at the hand of God as they saw their world destroyed. Even their own domain deep beneath the earth in hidden places was riven by the violence. Terrified, they could feel God's hand reaching down for them and sensed the coming of Michael, to chain and drag them to the Abyss yawning wide to receive their blackened souls. They screamed in anger and hatred and grieved the loss of their children who had been conceived in contempt of God and as malice towards man. The crushing of their heads had come.

But it was only a prelude.

16

The Simulcast

Art has two constant, two unending concerns:
It always meditates on death and thus always creates life.
All great, genuine art resembles and continues
The Revelation of St John.

—Boris Pasternack

Secrecy involves a tension which,
At the moment of revelation,
Finds its release.

—Georg Simmel

At the ripe old age of 82 Vitruvius Affluveum felt confident enough to release the mountain of collected and finalised notes to a team of European transcribers. The transcription teams simultaneously translated the 365 Nemrutium alloy pages from an English master text into German, Egyptian, French and Latin. This was done in honour of the archaeological pioneering nations. In addition it was translated into Turkish to whom the artifacts belonged. The database was burned onto mini disks and added to a full text that was published by a separate publications team working alongside BP2 under Llewelyn Loess' communications team. The Affluveum Codex published in six languages sold over 80 million copies during the first week after publication.

Before the transcription was complete however, and following twenty months of negotiations by various UN teams and different foreign governments, a first complete public reading was announced. It was to be presented by Llewelyn Loess and various BP2 team leaders rostered on for the reading, as well as selected world celebrities and politicians, at a televised simulcast and cyber-reading live from the Vatican on the 26th of September 2020 as well as five other locations, including the Temple Mount in Jerusalem, the new Twin Towers sanctuary in New York City, and Istanbul's Blue Mosque.

The marathon read was broken into chapters with fifteen-minute breaks every quarter hour to allow for televised and cyber commentary, reaction and reportage, day and night during the simulcast. The English reading was shared by several nations and religions. Subsequent partial readings were conducted at various universities, in the Louvre, Paris, and the House of Lords, London, after 2022. The whole world waited to hear what voice of the ancient past had to say and what insights would be revealed about human history. Most of the scholars had a rudimentary understanding of the content, but only the triumvirate of Affluveum, Tang and Ormond, as well as Loess, had a comprehension of the translated whole.

Vitruvius attended at St Peters Basilica, but did not speak during the broadcast. Ever dismissive and uninterested in public attention, he stood at the front and placed the text of the modern English translation onto the podium of St Peter's and turned toward Loess motioning him to commence. Viewers all over the world waited with baited breath. It reminded old timers of the Apollo 11 landing of July 1969, "That's one small step for [a] man, one giant leap for mankind."

With Italian Pope Innocent III and the UN Secretary General Dr. Xavier Alabi of Zimbabwe behind him, Professor Llewelyn Loess cleared his throat. He paused for what seemed an eternity, glanced over at Vitruvius, a huge smile on his bear-like face. Llewelyn Loess' large fleshy hands gripped both sides of the podium. He began, slowly, carefully, enunciating each of the first three words in his beautiful Welsh accent, savouring each syllable.

"THERE . . .

"WAS . . .

" SILENCE . . . ,"

he paused, and continued,

" . . . in heaven."

The Affluveum Codex proved to be a poetic historicity that shocked the scientific, religious, academic and historic worlds.

Nothing prepared them for the story that emerged. It fuelled academic debate for the next fifty years. Speculation alone about who might have written the Codex—Enoch, Noah, Methusaleh—or how it was made, generated thousands of books, and influenced the main world religions of Christianity, Islam and Judaism, as well as impacting world politics.

17

The Nephaliim Undone

When an evil spirit comes out of a man,
It goes through arid places seeking rest
And does not find it.

    —MATTHEW 12:43

Drawing breath to con-tem-plate
The battering of Body,
Soul,
And embittered Heart,
Swam he toward the edge;
Only to find there dryness of Spirit
No purpose, no horizon and
Plunging back in-to
The en-folding embrace of Darkness.

    —JOHN STRINGER

I nearly drowned in the wrath that consumed your First Age . . .
As I had endured his fowl stench so far, I clung to him . . .
And trailed in his wake through the vile waters . . .
And with my last burst of life, I cast the rank corpse
Away from me and into the sliding fire and shadow.

    —J. R. R. TOLKIEN, THE LORD OF THE RINGS

AFTER THE WATERS WRESTLED and undid the nephaliim, they cried out. Their voices were snuffed out like a dying vapour and their bodies were buried deep in mud, stone and water. All their arrogant flesh perished absolutely. Born of the Fallen Ones, they were eternal and, although their spirits left their bodies, they had no soul. Their disembodied spirits raced up toward the heavens but could not proceed through the atmospheres of the earth where the great canopy had been. They panicked, for they were caught between, and descended again in great whirling invisible schools. They found only water beneath them and waters above them which they greatly feared. They could not rest.

The spirits of the nephaliim twisted and turned speeding to and fro like hungry birds that could not alight. There was no ground. They had to fly continually. This was their judgement until the Coming and they laboured like this between the earth and the heavens. But afterward when the waters abated they came down to the earth, but could find no form and could not settle or rest anywhere. They were like insects that can never cease flying.

Exposed and naked, the nephaliim suffered greatly in this state for they could no longer express themselves. They were empty spirits eternally and ever hungry and unable to rest. God dispossessed them of the earth where they had inhabited and ruled with such cruelty. They were neither of heaven; instead, they were lost in a limbo of their own undoing. These, the spirits of the nephaliim cast adrift, were no longer "nephaliim," simply "~haliim," because their neph–their flesh–was destroyed. They will be called in various tongues of later men "sair" or "daimon"–the disembodied sons of the Fallen Ones. Ever afterward, until the Coming, they will torment men, like flies gathered in their multitudes on a bloody corpse. With the utmost desperation the unclean spirits of the haliim will try to break back into the world of men, clustered together in desolation and loss. Afterward, they will gather about men and cling to them hungering for abodes in which to dwell. So hungry will they be to feel again, they will feed off the emotions of men. Only in the minds of men when windows are opened will the haliim find rest from their continual astral wandering. Blown aimlessly by nothing and everything in an unworld between physical and spiritual but of neither, they will exist in a non-place where there is no emotion, no reference, no ethos of anything created. They will see and hear and comprehend in sharp focus the created reality of man but this will only add to their torment. They will zero in on men and their thoughts and this will be the only anchor they have in the great spiritual expanse in which they are trapped.

God acted, and glorified man above the haliim. All the bodies of men of that final generation in the one-hundred-and-twentieth year were destroyed. Their souls were flushed away into Sheol. There men will stay, as shades, until the Coming of one who will come to them, as Nu had done. This is a great grace from God, for every living soul of man from that time, will be met by the Great One, but that is a tale of another time.

> He who learns must suffer.
> And even in our sleep pain that cannot forget
> Falls drop by drop upon the heart,
> And in our own despair, against our will,
> Comes wisdom to us by the awful grace of God.[1]

As men were swept away for keeping and redemption, the haliim crept about in the earth in dark and lonely places like crawling insects through the dust of the earth. They sought men out, whispering to them, living vicariously through men whom earlier they had forced to serve them. They were consumed with contempt like sodden shipwrecked souls grabbing desperately at sinking life rafts in a darkened sea of gloom, despair and fear.

After the Waters, men will walk freely on the earth and the haliim will envy them. They will long to regain bodies but God will keep them bound out, just as Apollyon is bound away in the deepest fastness.

In time Sa-Tan and His Watchers and their children, the hoards of haliim, will take to creating delusions. They deceived men about their presence. In darkness they were able to come near to men and whisper to their heart and soul. Some men worshipped them, fooled that the spirits that spoke were divine, and above men, when they were not. The haliim will seek passions from which to feed. Anger, fear, pain, despair, murder, resentment, bitterness, un-forgiveness, hatred; all these things they will hunger to have. They will feed off these things in men, drawing near to traumas, invading the spirits of men when windows are opened. They will attempt to overcome a man and inhabit his body through his mind. Where one succeeds, other haliim will rush, cramming in, selfishly clinging to the human, like maggots crawling through a carcass. This will make some men insane. The lost haliim will only find expression and actuality through the body of men by filling minds with voices.

---

1. Aeschylus, *Agamemnon*.

They can do nothing of themselves, but only as they are able to persuade men to do on their behalf. This will be done through long whisperings in the night, nurtured with subterfuge and patient seduction, united with the evil in their human hosts.

For outside a man's spirit, the haliim are pained by the coldness of death. They have not the blanket and shelter of blood. Evil and the juice of the Bloodred Tree shot through their wicked souls like chill winds on naked skin. They will seek human souls in which to live, to avoid the chills of evil that will wrack them continually. The haliim will follow humans down through generations, seeking the susceptible and those who encourage openings to them. Then they will crawl in and abide there, finding rest from their void. And so family lines will be polluted by their influence until the Coming.

The haliim will never sleep. They have no physical body and are isolated from all the senses and experiences they have enjoyed as nephals. This was the beginning of their punishment, because they had abused and corrupted all flesh that God had made for good. God denied them physical habitations. So they fed off the emotions and passions of men, like parasitic plants on a stout tree. It was all of their own doing. God simply closed doors to where they had dwelt and they found themselves locked out in the cold of their own evil selfishness.

They will become wasted and drawn in their dimension and their evil hearts will grow blacker ever still. They were empty howling things and God looked at them like creeping crawling insects. God held them in their limbo between heaven and earth to await the great fire at the end of things, when their fathers, death, and Apollyon will be no more.

The haliim greatly fear the Coming of the Man promised from the very beginning to Sa-Tan in Phirst, the One who is to be. Those old nephals are terrified, for they know that man will utterly destroy them and unleash a judgement upon them like the Waters of Nu. They know they will be cast into the Yawning Abyss, to join their fathers the Watchers, the East Gate seraphim and the Cherub who fell. But for a little while they remained, for God had other concerns upon the earth. There was a ship and eight people inside with the seed of all creation.

The ship of Nu grounded on a level mountain peak in the land of Urartu. On the three-hundred-and-seventy-seventh day after the Waters burst forth, God opened the great door in the ship, which he had sealed. Light flooded through the skies and warmed Nu and his family.

They stood in awe at the sight. The old sky was gone and the heavens were painted a beautiful blue. Pieces of the sky drifted through the sky as clouds. This was a sight no men had ever seen before. They marvelled at the golden light that came from the sky that bathed their skin in gold. It was pleasant and warmed their blood and was a great wonder; this fascinated the family of Nu for many years. But later, after man had come down from the mountain, and in his foolishness, he worshipped the golden light as a god and forgot again the LoGoi.

Nu's sons and daughters came out and Nu went before them a way and knelt down. Piling up rocks he made an altar and Sem brought the young of several kinds to his father. These, Nu slaughtered as he had been shown and roasted them on fire. He piled them up in the same way his ancestor Oné and the first people had done. The smoke went up and it pleased God. This was the first thing a man did after the door was opened and man stepped again onto the cleansed earth. The first act of life was a giving back to God in death.

Nu offered up to God a great gift offering on stones and the families ate before the LoGoi, under the new blue sky.

There was silence in heaven for this was the end of the first of the seven millennia.

Nu and his family then released all the creatures within the opened ship. The pens and cages and stalls were opened and God awoke all the animals from their deep slumber. They moved out in their orders: the birds and flying things into the air; the great land beasts of the soil. The creatures moved down the great mountain of Urartu that is north of Van. But Nu and his family, all eight, stayed with the ship a year. They lived in the great ship as a home peacefully with some of their animals until it became too cold. When God sent snow, they followed the animals down the mountain and came in to valleys greatly changed and which they did not recognise. The land was scarred and torn in recognition of God's rent heart. Ragged mountains and scarps dotted the landscape. Great rivers rushed down onto the plain and out into the collecting seas and lakes gradually drawing away into their places. Everywhere great waterfalls thundered as the waters found their ways from the high places of the earth.

The land was scarred and torn, scoured beyond recognition. Nu's family marvelled at God's power and what He had done with the waters. Soaring mountain ranges had been thrust up under the waters during the deluge and these changed all vistas and horizons. The earth had groaned. Great landmasses had broken up and slid on the skin of the earth. As the waters drained and gathered, they settled into basins and became the great lakes and seas of the world.

After a year the land and the waters were in unity and balanced in their places of rest.

God brought weather. Nu and his family had not seen this before. They experienced rain, cloud and storms; light and dark; the temperature changed according to the seasons as the earth rotated on her axis offset by the cataclysm. Men began to record and set times by these changes, and learned the natures of the storehouses of heaven, and the treasures of the earth.

Nu and his family wondered at night, for they could see all the teraphim in the heavens as great lights that Apollyon and the Watchers had undone. They were beautiful and forever afterward caused men to marvel and wonder at God, although some foolishly worshipped them.

Nu and his family, Jahf, Sem, and Hamaa and their wives were content. Their lives were filled with wonder and business, and they came down into the mountainous region beneath Urartu and settled in its high valleys. In later years their children spread out from there in prosperity and happiness.

In the second year after the Waters, Nu planted a fruiting vine in the foothills and gathered and fermented his first harvest. One season he became drunk and fell down in his tent naked. A son of Hamaa came by and saw him exposed and mocked his grandfather while he slept and the young man posed and did lewd things. This boy was called Kainos, after Oné's first son, for he was the first son of Hamaa after the Waters abated. Jahf and Sem chased their nephew Kainos away and took a blanket and covered their father, and restored his respect.

This was an evil thing toward Nu by his grandson, for Nu was a venerable and wise old man and the father of the earth. When he heard of it he was very angry. He banished Kainos from his place and cursed him. Kainos and his family were sent away for the act had brought shame upon the clan because it was contemptuous of Nu. Kainos was cursed to be a servant to all his brothers through the generations because of this contempt for his elders, and so it was down through the line of Kainos the younger, as it had been for Kainos the elder, the first son of the earth.

After coming down from the great mountain of Urartu where the ship had come to ground, Nu built a settlement. He and his sons and his sons' sons–the Nu-oi–cut a tunnel through solid rock back into a hillock where they had built their settlement. At the end of the tunnel, Nu sunk a shaft twelve feet deep–one foot down for each of the Watchers that sunk from heaven, as well as the twelve months they had all been entombed in the great ship during the cleansing of the ground. Sem make a delicate wooden box and into this ten-inch container–an inch for each finger of humanity–Nu placed his most valued item from the ship, the beautiful book of metal cast by his great-grandfather En-Ocha. It had 365 leaves containing the ancient prophesies and the truth of what had happened in the beginning, during the time of the ancestors, and of things to come, that Unos had shown En-Ocha in visions and dreams. Toward the end of his life, Nu buried the sacred book and its box in a square hole at the bottom of the shaft and covered it with a square lid with his seal upon it. The seal was crafted by one of Sem's sons and showed Nu with his long white beard, the beard he grew after the Waters and did not cut so that it touched the ground. The glyph showed Nu holding a gazelle and a lamb, the great farmer and master of all the wild animals that he had saved by building the great ship. After the stone lid was fitted over Sem's wooden box, Nu poured sacred soil from off Urartu Mountain over the lid and then filled the shaft with water. It served as a holy well at the end of the tunnel cut through the solid rock by the Nu-oi, speaking of the Twelve, the fingers and acts of man, the days of the year and the acts of God.

Nu and Nu-Anna were happy and had many other children. Sem, Hamaa and Jahf had many children also and as the years went, they moved off in their clans to establish villages and settlements of their own, and to trade with each other.

After Nu-Anna died, Nu died soon after, and his sons buried their bones in a cave up near the ship. Their vital organs were reverently interred in two metal urns constructed by Sem and two grandchildren made crude clay heads (one for Nu and one for Nu-Anna) that were fitted into the neck of each urn to seal the contents. The urns of their beloved father and mother were lowered down into the well until they settled above the square lid under which Nu had sealed the sacred family book. Over the entrance to the tunnel where the well lay, Jahf and Hamaa built a huge gateway. They erected two megalithic well-cut stones and settled a stone lintel on top. Jahf, Hamaa and Sem burned Nu's settlement and dug the ashes into the soil, dispersed all his animals among the family, and then went their ways.

A generation later, Jahf, Hamaa and Sem were also buried up by the ship and their vital organs added to their own urns in turn, stopped with clay figural heads, and lowered into the sacred well, to join their parents—the first family of the earth after the rebirth of the earth after the Waters. Soil was poured in from above to cover the urns–five in all–and a circular stone lid was fitted over the top of the well to seal the family in the sacred shaft filled with water.

Foolishly, the site developed into a cult complex, and the family were worshipped as gods in the sacred well. Eventually, however, it was forgotten and people worshipped the stone megaliths Jahf and Hamaa had erected as gods. But these fell in an earthquake and the site was covered over by sand delivered by the frequent sand storms that blew in from the plains. The ship too became a sacred place and a byword for "going up to seek Unos" in the place where Nu and Nu-Anna had lived. But God sealed it in ice, to preserve the great ship as a sign for the End Times when it would be released from the ice for men to find. That place became in later years the mythological "homeland" of the first generations raised by Nu and Nu-Anna, and passed in to legend. Ever afterward people looked up to the sacred mountains of Nu, and many climbed the steep mountain looking for the ship, but it was not found.

The generations passed and the animals prospered and men grew in peace. The haliim had not yet learned how to whisper to men but they watched and envied them constantly as they flew through out the earth looking for rest.

But Sa-Tan and his servants the Fallen Ones were not idle. Sa-Tan established his throne on the Plain of Shinar beneath the valleys of Nu west of old Phirst. Eventually men came down to there, migrating down between the two great rivers as their generations grew and their children spread out.

The bodies of the Watchers of Flesh, who had gathered the light of their brothers into themselves so that they had form, perished in the deluge. They gathered their spirits around Sa-Tan's seat. He sent them throughout the earth and they took such kingdoms over the skin of the earth and under the earth, as they were allocated–great principalities. The unembodied Watchers on the earth preyed upon and bullied the spirits of the haliim like hawks raking through schools of bats aloft in twilight skies. They oppressed their offspring into armies of millions and gathered them into masses across the invisible kingdoms of the earth. All was under Sa-Tan, that is, Shemgazi, the Red Dragon, through fear and power whose throne was the Middle Kingdom that lay at the heart of the connected principalities of the earth. He lorded it over the disembodied Fallen Ones and the haliim hordes their sons, those old haliim, which the six Watchers of Flesh had created on the earth. All plotted and schemed, conceiving myriads of evil plans. They waited for men to come down from the mountains after the waters had abated, ever fearing the coming of the One destined to undo them all.

Deep within the earth, below old Phirst, the juice of the Bloodred Tree seeped into the inner recesses of the ground and was lost to its core as the earth gathered it back into its inner holy self where fire purified the veins of life.

18

Epilogue

Seraph: *Did you always know?*
The Oracle: *Oh no. No, I didn't. But I believed . . . I believed.*

—The Matrix: Revolutions

Every end is a new beginning.

Following the Vatican simulcast and the publication of the English translation of the Affluveum Codex, Vitruvius felt his life work was done. He packed up the conservancy in Istanbul. He ordered the disassembly of the official scholarly teams and closed the Affluveum Institute amid hails of academic horror. He signed over royalties and the publication rights to many of his writings to a variety of archaeological and historical institutes he trusted and admired. His notebooks went to the Nicholson Museum of Sydney University, the Affluveum Codex and Moses' Coffee Pots remained housed at the archaeological museum of Istanbul University where all humanity could view them. Other scholars would now add their science to the findings over their generations.

As a lifelong bachelor, he retired to Adelaide in Australia–a land he had always loved–with a favourite British bulldog called Achilles (who would never heel). He kept a breeding clutch of now rare Eurasian pygmy shrews allowed him by the Australian Government. He grew blood red roses, was heaped with international honours and accolades, and died within eighteen months of the Vatican simulcast. He was eighty-four.

Glossary

Al-Algar/Nim-Roda (of the North), a third-generation king of the Great Plain

Algaroi/Ceratopsia, a tribe of men

Alsoi, a tribe of men that could fly by contrivance

Ammel-Galanna (from the West), a fifth-generation king of the Great Plain

Ammel-Uanna (in the South), a fourth-generation king of the Great Plain

Amoth-Agga-Og, nephal of JNN

Amoth-Uma-Enom, nephal of PaZuZu

Andraemonoi, a tribe of men

Andraemon, a man of the Myrrion, killer of Fafnir-Amon

Ankylosoi, a tribe of men

Anna-Numanna-Ham, rebellious wife of Hamaa

Aoo-umm-aazzaootha, the greatest of God's creatures, a majestic marine beast

Apatasaurs, creature of the Great Plain

Apollyon (Abysso), the rebellious Cherubim of Song, East Gate

Arch-aeopteryx, ancient feathered bird

Argolis, a nephaliim high place

Arook-Anuth-Amun-ni-Tagasar, a nephal of JNN

Ashak-Leviathan-Un-Zamzummin-Osh-Akalok-Nephiliim, literally "Place where the Great One was Humbled by Osh the Nephal," the killing spot of the great marine creature Aoo~

Auroch, a large and dangerous prehistoric ox

Glossary

Axel-rod-ichthys, a blue-red scaled marine creature
Azarel-e-ath-Tigath-ti-Gasamon, a nephal in the time of Nu
AZaZel, a fallen Watcher, and region of the Great Plain

Ba-Bel, a later city on the Plain of Shinar
Blood Men, see *Kainoi*

Cera-Tops, animals husbanded by Jahf, son of Nu
Ceratopsians, animals of the Great Plain
Cerboroi, a tribe of men
CHaRun, a fallen Watcher, and region of the Great Plain
Cherubim, first order of angels, Gabriel, Raphael, Michael, Apollyon
Christine Garrat, New Zealand academic who found the floor glyph
Coelophysis, creature of the Great Plain
Crypto-clidfoi, a long-necked marine serpent with large fins

Dimetrodons, a toothed lizard with a large spinal sail
Dino-hippus, a horse-like creature, kept in herds by Hamma son of Nu; also: *meso~*, *para~* and *proto-hippus*; and *equus*.
Diplodocus, a long-necked sauropod with a huge tail
Dorcan affair, historic controversy between Turkish authorities and James Melllart over artifacts associated with Catal Huyuk
DRKaVac, a fallen Watcher, and region of the Great Plain
Dunkleosteus, a savage-toothed eel
Du-Muzi, a sixth-generation king of the Great Plain

Eastmen, a tribe of men
Eduli, painful parasites
Eqqus, a horse-like creature

Enme-Du-Ranki, a ninth-generation king of the Great Plain

En-Meush-Um-Galanna, a seventh-generation king of the Great Plain

En-Ocha, third-generation Nu-oi, great-grandfather of Nu

Ensi-Pazi-Anna, an eighth-generation king of the Great Plain

Eva, the first woman, wife of Oné

Eurhino-delphoi, marine creatures

Fafnir-Amon, a nephal killed by Andraemon

Gabriel, Cherubim of Words

Geryon, a place with large pack dogs that attacked Heracleos

Gib-Ral-Tar, a great land bridge to the extreme west of the Great Plain

GoRgoNos, a fallen Watcher, and region of the Great Plain

Great Fissure, a great seam around the skin of the earth

Great Man, a legendary future vengeance from womankind against the Watchers

Great Plain, the main geography of men in the first ten generations

Hadoi, a tribe of men

Haliim, disembodied nepahliim spirits after the Waters

Hamaa, second son of Nu

Hamaa-Oz-Olloc, chief wife of Hamaa

Hamaa-Umzalloch, a rebellious wife of Hamaa

Hemenoi, a tribe of men

Heracleos, a legendary nephal of GoRgoNos

Hilluma-Ham, a rebellious wife of Hamaa

Hu-Man, a man king

Hydra, a legendary conflation of remnant sauropods killed by Heracleos.

Ibenox and **ibex**, stout-horned ox-sheep of the mountains

INCuBu, a fallen Watcher, and region of the Great Plain

Jahf, first son of Nu

Jahf-Azmollec-Un-Anna (Jahf-Anna), chief wife of Jahf

Jahf-Sumanna, a rebellious wife of Jahf

James Mellaart discoverer of Catal Huyuk

Jerome Ladsen, senior archaeologist who excavated the megaliths at Track Alley

Kainoi, The Blood Men, a tribe of men, descendents of Kainos

Kainos, the first son of Oné, ancestor of the Blood Men/Kainoi

Kaz-Pian, a great sea to the east

Kronos, a legendary nephal

Lam-Ech, fifth-generation Nu-oi, father of Nu

Leaping Fish, creatures of the sea

Llewelyn Loess, Welsh academic, head of BP2's communications unit

Mammut, an elephant-like creature, also *mastodon*

Mastodon, an elephant-like creature, also *mammut*

Men of Oné, a tribe of men

Men of Phirst, a tribe of men

Meso-hippus, a horse-like creature

Ma-Goth, the only nephal to see the ship of Nu

Methu-Saleh, fourth-generation Nu-oi, grandfather of Nu

Michael, Cherubim of Warriors

Moscops, creature of the Great Plain

Mononykus, creature of the Great Plain

Mt Hermon, landing place of the Watchers

Myrrion, the sanctuary of Andraemon and the Great Mothers

Notharctus, creature of the Great Plain

Nemea, a nephaliim high place

Nemrut Dag, Vitruvius Affluveum"s career excavation site in central Turkey

Nemrutium, the unknown Codex metal alloy, named after Nemrut Dag

Nephaliim, nephal, a race of sterile man-gods spawned by women and Watchers

Nu, Builder of the great ship, retrospective namesake of the Nu-oi, son of Lam-Ech

Nu-Anna, wife of Nu

Nu-mastafoi, large hyena-like dogs domesticated by Nu that protected him

Nu-oi, the tribe of Nu

Oné [Onay], the first man, a son of God and friend of Unos, husband of Eva

Onés, the first human city, built by Oné, west of Phirst on the Great Plain

Oryx, the great river of the Valley of Nu

Osh, a nephal

Ox-Muta, a chief man of the valley of Nu

Ox Hammer, a great battering ram fashioned by Ox-Muta

Oviraptors, colorful songful feathered creatures

Paraceratherium, a huge camel-like horse

PaZuZu, a fallen Watcher and region of the Great Plain

Peradons, great flying creatures

Pely-cosaurs, a sail-lizard similar to a Dimetrodon

Phirst, the Garden of God, first home of Oné and Eva, principal home of the Nu-oi

Platybelodons, creature of the Great Plain

Proto-ceratopsians, animals of the Great Plain

Pteradons, majestic winged creatures

Pterodactyls, majestic winged creatures

Pterasaurs, majestic ancient birds like pelican-bats

Para-hippus, a horse-like creature

Phirst, the first place men were, in God's Garden; later the name of a region

Proto-hippus, a horse-like creature

Raphael, Cherubim of Watching

Raptormen, a tribe of men

Rathma-Rama-Zod-Akon (Akon), a nephal

Rham-pho-hycoi

Sa-Tan (the), also:

Shining One/Red Shining One
    Red Dragon
    Red Serpent

Snake Crusher

See also: *Watchers, Shemgazi*

Sem, third son of Nu

Sem-Anna-Hill-Ashak, Sem's chief wife, redeemed Kainoi

Seraphim, second order of angels between cherubim and teraphim

Shemgazi, rebellious seraphim Watcher of Apollyon, East Gate; see Sa-Tan

Shinar, a great plain south of Van

Solmantaloc-Jahf, rebellious wife of Jahf

Sons of TiaMat, legendary nephals

Glossary 155

Stegosaur, a rare herbivore with huge plates down it's spine

Steno-pterygius, marine creatures

Styracs, a tribe of men

Tané Megaloi., gigantic trees of the forest

Tenontosaur, creature of the Great Plain

Teraphim, third order of angels

The Four Great Creatures, created entities closest to the Throne of God

The Elders that are to be, 24 men: 12 Apostles and 12 endogenous Tribal Chiefs of the ancient Habiru (Hebrews)

The Twelve, the twelve seraphim Watchers released by Michael, including Shemgazi; *Watchers.*

Titans, legendary nephals

Theropoda, creature of the Great Plain

TiaMat, a fallen Watcher, and region of the Great Plain

Urartu, a mountainous land near Phirst

U-Bar-Tutuy/Zi-U-Sudra, last chief Hu-Man of the Great Plain, tenth-generation.

Unos, the Faithful One, the LoGoi, God who visits man

Umaduzi-Oz-Olloc, rebellious wife of Jahf

Van, the region containing the Valley of Nu

Vast Expanse, extremes of the Great Plain

Velociraptor, swift feathered creatures

Watchers (the), fallen seraphim of Apollyon's East Gate

    ABRaXaS, a fallen Watcher, and region of the Great Plain
    AZaZeL, a fallen Watcher, and region of the Great Plain

CHaRuN, a fallen Watcher, and region of the Great Plain
DRKaVaC, a fallen Watcher, and region of the Great Plain
GoRgoNoS, a fallen Watcher, and region of the Great Plain
INCuBu, a fallen Watcher, and region of the Great Plain
JNN, a fallen Watcher, and region of the Great Plain
PaZuZu, a fallen Watcher, and region of the Great Plain
Shemgazi, captain of the Twelve
TaRTaRos, a fallen Watcher, and region of the Great Plain
TiaMaT, a fallen Watcher, and region of the Great Plain
ZeMu, a fallen Watcher, and region of the Great Plain

Watchers of Flesh, six only of The Twelve who took physical form

ABRaXaS
CHaRuN
DRKaVaC
INCuBu
JNN
PaZuZu

Worgm, a diminished nephal at the end of its life in the roots of a mountain

Yaheli and **Yesom**, guardian Warrior angels of the West Gate

Yawning Abyss, place of judgement for Apollyon, the Watchers, and seraphim of the East Gate

Zamzummin, a coastal race of men

Zebubas, painful parasites

ZeMu, a fallen Watcher, and region of the Great Plain

Zhou Tang, academic of Peking University, a member of Trinity

www.ingramcontent.com/pod-product-compliance
Lightning Source LLC
Chambersburg PA
CBHW051931160426
43198CB00012B/2111